Margaret Cooper

FRANCIS FRITH'S

COLLECTED MEMORIES OF BUCKINGHAMSHIRE

THE FRANCIS FRITH COLLECTION

www.francisfrith.com

Collected Memories of
Buckinghamshire

Inspired by The Francis Frith Collection®

THE FRANCIS FRITH COLLECTION

www.francisfrith.com

First published in the United Kingdom in 2013
by The Francis Frith Collection®

Paperback edition 2013 ISBN 978-1-84589-732-1

British Library Cataloguing in Publication Data

Collected Memories of Buckinghamshire

The Francis Frith Collection®
6 Oakley Business Park, Wylye Road,
Dinton, Wiltshire SP3 5EU
Tel: +44 (0) 1722 716 376
Email: info@francisfrith.co.uk

www.francisfrith.com

Printed and bound in Great Britain
Contains material sourced from responsibly managed forests

Front Cover: HIGH WYCOMBE, Frogmore Square 1921 70607t
Frontispiece: AYLESBURY, Market Square 1901 47462xt

*Every attempt has been made to contact copyright holders of
illustrative material. We will be happy to give full acknowledgement in future editions for
any items not credited. Any information should be directed to The Francis Frith Collection.*

*The colour-tinting in this book is for illustrative purposes only,
and is not intended to be historically accurate*

*AS WITH ANY HISTORICAL DATABASE, THE FRANCIS FRITH
ARCHIVE IS CONSTANTLY BEING CORRECTED AND IMPROVED, AND
THE PUBLISHERS WOULD WELCOME INFORMATION ON OMISSIONS
OR INACCURACIES*

Collected Memories of Buckinghamshire – A Dedication

This book has been compiled from a selection of the thousands of personal memories added by visitors to the Frith website and could not have happened without these contributions. We are very grateful to everyone who has taken the time to share their memories in this way. The combination of all these personal stories provides a wonderful insight into British life and this book is therefore dedicated to everyone who has taken the time to participate in the Frith Memories project.

Each memory is personal to the writer yet the pictures painted are part of a shared inheritance, reminders of a life that so many people still cherish in their memories. For others, these memories will provide an insight into a way of life that has now vanished.

In the current uncertain times it is comforting to find so many stories full of human warmth which bring back happy memories of 'the good old days'. We hope that everyone reading this book will find stories that amuse and fascinate whilst at the same time be reminded of why we feel affection for Britain and what makes us all British.

Francis Frith always expressed the wish that his photographs be made available to as wide an audience as possible and so it is particularly pleasing to me that by creating the Frith website we have been able to make this nationally important photographic record of Britain available to a worldwide audience. Now, by providing the Share Your Memories feature on the website we are delighted to provide an opportunity for members of the public to record their own stories and to see them published (both on the website and perhaps in our books), ensuring that they are shared and not lost or forgotten.

We hope that you too will be motivated to visit our website and add your own memories to this growing treasure trove – helping us to make it an even more comprehensive record of the changes that have taken place in Britain in the last 100 years and a resource that will be valued by generations to come.

John M Buck
Managing Director
www.francisfrith.com

CHESHAM, High Street c1955 C81004

Contents

My lovely childhood at Chalfont St Peter

I wonder how many people from Chalfont St Peter remember the Rose and Crown, a Benskins pub. My father owned it from 1946 until 1950. There was also the Kings Head, which was on the corner of Joiners Lane. Of course if you look for either of them now you won't find them, the area is covered by the dual carriageway and roundabout, although when I lived in Chalfont as a child there were hardly any cars going through it. My father said that because there were quite a few pubs in the village in those days the rivalry for customers was pretty fierce, and he had to think of all different ways to get custom. The pub had an old stable block behind it which he turned into a club room. He hired this out for functions and started an Ancient Order of Buffaloes Lodge. Dad did catering for the local gymkhanas and the bar for the dances held at the hospital. He also arranged outings to Goodwood races and local darts team matches.

I remember there was an elderly lady tramp around village then called Lottie. She used to pick a pub once a week for a handout, so she managed to get a free bite to eat every day. Another lady that lived opposite the Rose and Crown, in a small row of cottages, was my music teacher, her name was Miss Rissbeanie. I had a friend whose father Mr Isles owned the shoe-mender's shop in the village, she had a goat called 'Snowy' that was like a pet dog to her, and she used to walk about with it on a lead.

Some of the people I remember from the village in those days were Mr Blatner the baker, Mr Drewett the barber, and Mr Honeyball who had a sweet shop. I remember some of my school teachers as well, they were Miss Ruth, Miss Golding and Miss LaMay who was the headmistress. We had a tea monitor at the school who would stand beneath a shelf which was high up on the cloakroom wall and had a gas ring on it. On this gas ring would perch a kettle filled with water, and the tea monitor would call for a teacher when it was boiling to make their tea. So much for Health and Safety! Of course there was no TV at school in those days, the only thing then was Radio for Schools. For these lessons we had to walk from the school to the Scout Hut at the top of Gold Hill to have our lesson – come rain or shine.

We children had such a lot of freedom then. We would go up to Chalfont Heights and search the hedgerows to pick wild flowers (there were no laws to protect wild flowers then). I don't know if they still grow there but Green Hill Common was covered in harebells when I was a child. In the autumn we would scrump for apples and pick blackberries and hazelnuts. I remember one year when the fair came to the village and I made friends with one of the traveller children, she worked in the circus of the fair and gave us little demonstrations of tumbling on the playing field which was behind the pub. In the evening I used

CHALFONT ST PETER, High Street c1950   C524007

to sit with her in one of the old type of gypsy caravans and help her babysit some of the small children while their parents worked in the fair.

One of the favourite tricks of us village children in summer was to wade along the Misbourne River under the main road and blow loud raspberries as people walked over the bridge. I must admit it made a lovely loud echo!

I have lots of fond memories of my young days in Chalfont St Peter, but as the years go by I think the rose-tinted glasses get even more rosy.

Ivy Jones 230211

Life in Castle Street in the 1950s

My husband, Roger Watts, and his family lived in Castle Street in Aylesbury in the 1950s. On the right of this photograph of Castle Street is a figure standing outside their front door (number 15) which could be his mother or older sister Linda. The street was always free of cars in those days with only the doctor, who lived a few doors away, owning a vehicle. All the children in the street attended the local school, St Mary's, including a number of children with Italian fathers, thanks to the number of ex POWs who stayed in the area following the war. Playground language lessons included how to swear in two languages, which if overheard by the headmaster (who still lived in the school house on site) deserved a stroke with a cane across the legs – not very PC these days, but post-war children were made of sterner stuff! Although this part of old Aylesbury is now very much on the 'tourist trail', back in the 1950s the families living there were, on the whole, pretty close to the poverty line and it was difficult for parents to keep enough food on the table. Roger's house was not only home to their family of six but also had his grandfather and a lodger under the same roof. He slept in an attic room, with access from a ladder on the landing; it was cold in winter and hot in summer, but it gave him the opportunity to drop sprigs of ivy seeds onto the heads of passing neighbours without being noticed – hours of innocent fun!

Lesley Watts 345251

AYLESBURY, Castle Street c1955 A84037

My childhood in Loughton

Loughton was the village I grew up in. Now part of Milton Keynes, when I was young in the 1950s it was a lovely village surrounded by countryside and farmland. I grew up in Railway Cottages, sometimes known as Fog Cottages. Me and my friend Marlene used to sit on the fence, train numbering. I also remember going for walks in Linford Wood which was huge then and full of bluebells and primroses. In the summer we would also collect rosehips and blackberries. The mushrooms we collected in the field opposite our house were as big as dinner plates. The fields around the village were full of buttercups and daisies where we spent many a happy hour making daisy chains. Down the lane called Leys Lane, Bella Scott had her farm. Bella used to go through the village in a pony and trap. George Higgs was the postman and Frank Ebbs was the milkman. In the winter the village would flood and you couldn't get to the shop as the water was up to the shop door.

Jose Mabbutt 211261

My mother served the Queen!

I was born in Little Marlow in 1947 and lived three doors away from the village shop, which was then run by Miss Littlewood. When I was small I would go there to help her, weighing the sultanas, currants etc, and putting them into little blue bags.

My mum (Phyllis Wright) waited at table when Queen Elizabeth II came to visit Lord and Lady Ronaldshay at the manor house at Little Marlow, and I can also remember that when the England football team won the World Cup in 1966 the coach with all the players parked outside our house, whilst the players went to the manor house. My little bit of England is Little Marlow, although it's changed so much now, I still love it.

Liz Hughes 36791

> '*I can also remember that when the England football team won the World Cup in 1966 the coach with all the players parked outside our house, whilst the players went to the manor house.*'

Happy days at Fenny Stratford

In 1951, when I was about 4 or 5, my family moved from Water Eaton to Fenny Stratford. We lived with my gran, Mrs Gibson, in Church Street. My two brothers and myself attended the Salvation Army Sunday School nearby, we only lived a few doors away and felt grown up walking the few yards to it. I used to play the tambourine there (well, I used to rattle it about a bit). It was always nice and clean looking and felt homely. Next door was a 'house' that was used as a Catholic church, then next to that was our local fire brigade, all the kids used to gather round there when the siren went off on the council offices, knowing lots of men would be running like mad from wherever they worked – mainly as cooks in the brush factory in Victoria Road. They were all volunteer firemen, bless 'em! When I was old enough I used to go with my brothers to the County Cinema, which was just through a walkway opposite the house. My gran was one of the first people around to have a TV, on Coronation Day in 1953 there were people standing in her front room and sitting on her wall at the front with the window open and the sound turned up loud. A few years later, Mrs Dick started up a beetle drive, I went with her every week and helped her put the tables and chairs out, waiting for the people to arrive, 99% of them were ladies. Although I was young they were all local, so we all knew each other. It was always a very friendly evening, even now, over 50 years later, writing about it brings a smile to my face. Happy days and pleasant memories.

Margaret Hogg 90711

BLETCHLEY, Central Gardens c1955 B439022

BLETCHLEY, Bletchley Road 1961 B439056

Childhood memories of old Bletchley

During the Second World War my gran owned a grocery shop at 7 Stoke Road, Water Eaton and my grandad used to take a barrow round the streets selling slabs of salt. I remember looking out of my window (at about 3 or 4 years old) and watching the foxhounds meet on the green, it was a bit scary for me being so young. I also used to like walking up Stoke Road to see an old horse called Kit, he was very gentle and seemed to love people. When I was about 5 we moved to Church Street in Fenny Stratford, near 'old' Bletchley. I started at Bletchley Road School, then went on to Western Road, I was older then and could go out on my own (safely). I used to like going through the Central Gardens at Bletchley and seeing all the pretty flowers in little 'gardens' scattered in the lawns and the sunken 'bandstand', then all the tennis courts and pavilion, then out on to Bletchley Road. To the left was the cinema, with the open-air pool behind it, and to the right was Weatherhead's wooden record shop, then a garage and petrol forecourt (the 'AA' and 'RAC' signs outside it can be seen on the extreme left of photograph B439056 of Bletchley Road), and opposite was 'dear old Woollies'. Happy days! We'll never get those lovely peaceful, trouble-free, friendly days back, it's such a shame.

Margaret Hogg (née McCracken) 89301

The old pub on the corner

Built in 1780 as the Shoulder of Mutton, this thatched pub and its later brick-built extension at Bletchley was later known as the Three Trees. It closed in 1962 and was eventually demolished.

BLETCHLEY, Tree Square c1955 B439017

My first memory of this corner of Newton Road and Buckingham Road in Bletchley dates from the 1960s, when the brick-built extension of the pub seen in this view (the left hand side) was no longer standing, only the thatched cottage part remained. I used to love standing in front of it because it had a verandah and wooden railings like you would see in Western films, and my mum often had to drag me away. The pub by then was no longer in use, but the back wall still remains to this day. There would have been two reasons for us being at this corner in the 1960s, the first was that across in Shenley Road was our doctor's surgery in one of a row of brick-built cottages, the old front room being the waiting room with old wooden chairs; the second reason was that my family could only afford the bus fare one way, so we walked to town (going past the old pub) and then took a bus back home.

Alan Webb 204057

Reminiscing about Woburn Sands and Aspley Heath

I was born in north-west London. My first visit to Woburn Sands was about 1950 when my Uncle Ted and Aunt Ada moved there. They lived at The Dene, Aspley Hill. Aunt Ada did the housework for Mrs Russell, the owner of The Dene, and Uncle Ted drove a lorry for Marston Bricks. My school holidays were spent there, and I used to cycle all around the district. Then in 1955 my father Charles Batham bought Quarry Cottage in Sandy Lane, Aspley Heath. At that time there was no electricity or sewer. Mum cooked on a wood stove and we read by oil lamps. There was no TV and not even a radio. The toilet was the outhouse. I met my wife Barbara while travelling to work at Bletchley. We married in 1960 and in 1961 we purchased Quarry Cottage and half its land from my father, who built a bungalow on the remaining land which he called Charlesdene. It was then that electricity and sewers were connected. I worked at Woburn Engineering for a few years before emigrating to Western Australia in 1968. I still have many happy memories of the village, but no doubt many changes have taken place since I left it.

Roy Batham 4471

My young years at Castlefield, High Wycombe

I was born on 16th February 1953 in the front room of 49 Spearing Road at Castlefield, High Wycombe. I must have been lucky, as that was when Castlefield was posh, when the tally man was unarmed. All our school uniforms were bought on tick, but the company got paid eventually. I remember going swimming on the Rye wearing my woollen trunks that got bigger the longer you were in the pool, but Keep Hill was the place to be in those days when you were a teenager – many a young love was made or lost there. I can remember my first drink at the Van Inn when I was just 16. Now if I was 16 I would be fighting for a council house for me, the girlfriend and the kids, and if the front room of 49 Spearing Road came up I would turn it down. I wonder if anyone can else share my memories of Castlefield in my teenage years, such as Mrs Harley the sweet lady, Jerry the hairdresser at the back of the wool shop, the Co-op with your divvy number, the Castle when it had a snug, and sitting on that wall with your lemonade and crisps. Life was not easy then – but then maybe it was, after all. I am just glad I had my days in Castlefield and I really hope the young people there today can look back in 20 or 30 years and say "Yes, I liked my years in Castlefield". It would be a sad world if you regretted your childhood. I still live in Castlefield now. I did move to North Yorkshire for four years, but as they say – "You can take the man out of Wycombe, but you can't take Wycombe out of the man".

Ronnie Berry 22063

WENDOVER, Coldharbour Cottages, Tring Road 1899 44771

Watch your head!

My late sister, Daphne Hemmings, used to own Number 3 Coldharbour Cottage at
Wendover. I have fond memories of visiting her there and staying awhile in these
fascinating dwellings. You wouldn't want to be six-foot plus with the low doorways
plus the low oak beams on the ceilings, you would crack your head on them! If anyone
passed away upstairs their body had to be lowered through a trapdoor located in
the front bedroom in line with the front door. As a schoolboy during the Second
World War years I used to walk from Aylesbury to Wendover up Coombe Hill to the
Monument and in the war years (if my memory serves me correct) there were dummy
anti-aircraft guns all around the hills. In 1965 my wife, children and myself emigrated
to Australia. In 1993 we decided to have a trip back to the UK, staying with my sister in
Wendover for a short time. We decided to have a walk up Coombe Hill, which I hadn't
done since I was at school where as a boy it seemed like miles, this time it was like a
very short hike. Ah, Sweet Memories.

Peter Osbourne 243651

Stoke Poges – where I grew up

My mum and dad moved into the village of Stoke Poges in the 1930s into a new house in Rogers Lane and lived there for 66 years. My father was the village tailor, working from a workshop in the back garden, and was also a Special Policeman during and just after the Second World War. I was born in 1944 and spent my childhood playing in the fields which surrounded Stoke Poges, of which all but a few have now been built on.

I can remember many things from my childhood, including going up to the common and selecting our Christmas tree each year. When they first moved into Stoke Poges Mum and Dad were told they had the rights of the common, and this gave them the right to pick their own pea and bean sticks and a tree. Mum was very much into the history of Stoke Poges, and she later found out that this right came from heathland on the common which had been designated as a 'Poors Fuel Allotment' as a result of an Act of Enclosure in 1810. We also used to walk up to Brockenhurst Wood regularly to pick up wood for our fire, which was quite an expedition. Going shopping was different in those days, Mum used to write her list of things she needed in a book and drop it into Mrs Newell's grocery shop on Bells Hill, and then collect it later. We had a very good butcher in the village then, as well a Co-op and Jack Hearne the bike man, he used to mend bikes as well sell them. We also had the sweet and newsagent's shop, run by Tom Caldecot. I loved that shop, and spent my pocket money in there most weeks.

I remember our telephone number was Farnham Common 206 (the exchange was in Farnham Common), and that we were one of the few families to have an early television in the village – many people came in to our house to watch the Coronation of Queen Elizabeth II in 1953.

We used the village hall for many things but as a teenager I can remember going to the Fellowship Club on a Friday night for a disco. Dad and my brother used to supply the music and I always say my brother was one of the first DJs around, he always bought the top three records in the charts each week. I used to love going to the jumble sales in the hall as well, coming home with many a good find.

Vivien Halse (née Sowersby) 19701

'When they first moved into Stoke Poges Mum and Dad were told they had the rights of the common.'

Memories of Lane End and High Wycombe

I was born in the Shrubbery Nursing Home at High Wycombe in 1956 and grew up in Lane End, about 5 miles away. We lived in the Park Lane area, the eastern side of Lane End. Park Lane then mostly consisted of council houses built in the 1940s and 50s and we lived in Coronation Crescent, in a semi-detached 3-bedroom council house. These were not so much pebble-dashed as gravel-dashed houses, their outsides were sharp to the touch and the stones were a mix of white, pink and red colours. Our house was cold, and it only had one fireplace. My parents used a paraffin oil heater in the kitchen which they would also bring into the living room when it was very cold. The rooms never got cosy, so you sat by the fire, with your front melting and your back freezing. This helps explain why we took so few baths back then! Later my parents got one of those electric fires with bars that glow, and the cat sat too near it and singed her coat. The water was heated by a back boiler behind the fire in winter, and in the summer we used a copper water heater, a big cylinder with a tap. It was stood in the spare room across from the bathroom and it took ages to fill and empty it with a bucket.

Our back garden backed onto the farm of Mrs Archer, who kept pigs, and she apparently had a pet fox she would take for a walk but I never saw this. In about 1969 the fields from Mrs Archer's farm became 'the rabbit hutch estate' as we called it, due to the small backyard-type gardens of the houses that were built there, then about 10 years later the big red brick estate beyond that was built. Both houses on both estates then were council houses, but I expect that few are now.

My mother at one time worked as a cleaner for Jim Please and his family who ran the Old Sun pub. Mostly she left me on my own when she went to work, but she could not do that sort of thing nowadays. Dad worked in High Wycombe as a French polisher. He had grown up in Lane End, and was in the Lane End football and cricket teams in his younger days. He grew lots of fruit and vegetables, not just in our garden but he had several allotment plots as well. My mother always entered the local Horticultural Show each year with home-made wine, jam, cakes and handicraft, and also entered eggs from our own hens, while I entered jam tarts, a 'dinner plate garden', 'flowers in a jam jar' and 'flowers in a small paste jar'. I was also entered for fancy dress contests, oh how I hated that, but my mum loved making the costumes. In my later teens I went to the discos in the Village Hall. I went to school in Wheeler End, then later Bartholomew Tipping in Stokenchurch.

Shops and businesses in Lane End that I remember from my early years include Josephine's haberdashery shop opposite Harris the Bakers, and John Carr who had the grocers in the former Temperance Hotel. The Druces had the newsagent's. The Post Office was then next to the Old Sun pub and was small and dark, the public area was just the hall of a house. Then there was Ivy's hairdresser's, an ironmonger's, a butcher's, another grocer's shop opposite the Village Hall, and two shops in Park Lane. I remember we would take back Corona bottles to the one on the corner of what is now Archers Way. A grocer's van would also call to our street, and also the ice-cream van, where we would get a block of Neapolitan ice cream in the days before we had a fridge. I also used to get milk ice-lollies, the plastic sticks inside would have a model of Disney character on them, like Snow White or one of the seven dwarves model, which I would place in the front garden.

I remember that when I was young the River Wye ran through High Wycombe (it's now culverted), and our bus stop to catch the bus back home to Lane End after going shopping in the town was near it at the start of the Oxford Road. I remember the awful Woolworth's in High Wycombe, it was long and thin, turning back on itself, with lots of dark wood, and was very dingy. You had to stand holding your hand up at the counters to get served, often waiting ages as pushier people got served first. We had a Lyons corner shop tearooms in the town and I also remember Murrays, the big privately-owned department store in Wycombe, it had a fancy clock that travelled up and down while the stairs circled around it. It was a bit like a John Lewis store nowadays. I remember being taken to Wycombe to see Father Christmas, I guess that was probably in Murrays.

Vicky Searle 9591/57011

I had a Saturday job in High Wycombe's Woolworth store

Many years ago I had a Saturday job in the Woolworth's store in Church Street in High Wycombe (the shop with the large white awning seen on the right of this photograph), and at the end of the day one of my jobs was to oil the old and dingy wooden floor. I have two golden memories of the store. One is of being asked to turn the boxes of loose biscuits around and date-stamp them again a year hence, as they had already reached their 'best-before' date! The other is of working in the 'cage' where the soft drinks were kept. Being very thirsty on a hot day, I would carefully remove the foil-covered tops from Lucozade bottles, drink the top inch and then carefully replace the tops!

Donald Macdonald 23871

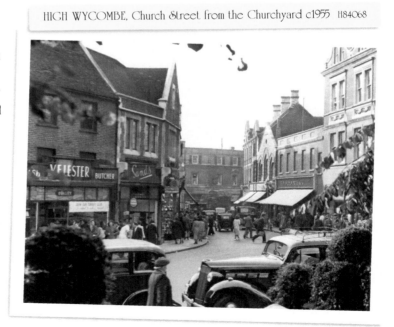

HIGH WYCOMBE, Church Street from the Churchyard c1955 H84068

Happy memories of High Wycombe

I was born in 1946 and grew up in the Micklefield district of High Wycombe, Melbourne Road to be exact. Oh what lovely memories I have! I'd go walking in Kings Woods with my father and pick bluebells, then we'd buy a threepenny bag of chips and walk home, watching the smoke spiral from the chimneys just before dark. I enjoyed going to Lord's and Gilbey's shops and buying sweets, having them cut out coupons from the ration book. We would take day trips to the seaside, everyone sang on the bus and passed the hat for the driver. I attended Netherwood School and St Bernard's Convent and we'd walk to The Rye to play lawn hockey and swing on the swings. My dad also used to take me rowing on the lake on The Rye and I'd catch tadpoles and bring them home in a bucket. My dad (Raymond Brown) used to play soccer for the Wycombe Wanderers and I used to go and watch the games...in the rain. I remember that we used to go to a fish and chip shop in High Wycombe that had a restaurant upstairs, it was by the 'Bull' bus stop across from the Murrays department store...to me that was the finest meal ever, aside from my gran's huge Sunday breakfasts. I was lucky, I had a great childhood. Even though I moved to the USA when I was twelve, part of me is still home in High Wycombe – and always will be.

Jo Makoul (née Brown) 135081

HIGH WYCOMBE, The Rye c1955 H84015

The Seven Stars Inn at Dinton

I was born in the public house called the Seven Stars Inn at Dinton. The date was the 5th November 1940. My godfather, then Doctor Ralph Gardiner, delivered me. He lived over the stile in the farm nearby. The pub was run by my Nan and her second husband Harry. Her first husband had run a cattle business at the rear of the pub, but unfortunately he died after a truck door hit him in the back. My mother Peggy lived at the pub with Nan (her mum) where, on arriving looking for digs, my father (Thomas Haydn Young) met her. The pub bar itself had two rooms, a small lounge in which I was born, and a large bar. Nan served from a small bar in the wall. Dominos was an almost nightly game in the pub and darts were played sometimes. The pub was a very atmospheric old building, it had very narrow stairs to the bedrooms, two small and one very big, which were used to house refugees from London during the Second World War. The Aylesbury Brewery lorry would come every Thursday and the men always had a pint outside before going on. The cellar was right under the front door entrance so was easy to stock into.

In those days we had a fish and chip van which visited the village each week, and of course there was a daily milkman. In 1949 Sir Carol Reed filmed 'Daughter of Darkness' in the village in which I was an 'extra', riding on a cart. I have a pretty decent photograph of that little take. All the villagers were swanning around like Hollywood stars for a few weeks.

In the mid 1940s my parents and I moved to a cottage at the bottom of the hill from the pub, but this never stopped me from going to the Seven Stars nearly every day to see my Nana, Ellen. After her death she was buried in the churchyard at Dinton church. She was a rough type of woman but was loved by all.

Dennis A Young 121791

> *'In 1949 Sir Carol Reed filmed 'Daughter of Darkness' in the village in which I was an 'extra', riding on a cart.'*

Memories of Orving

Around 1975-76 my father, Mr Hugh Jenkins, bought the house on the right of this photograph of Manor Road in Oving. The house was called Tinkers End and the phone number there was 268. I lived there until I married a local girl in 1981 and have lived in Aylesbury ever since. Around 1985 my father managed to buy the end cottage and my wife and I used this house as a temporary home for several months, as our own new house was not yet built. (My father later had the cottages made into one.) The first night I slept in the house was not a good one as I got no sleep, because all night long there was such a noise. In the morning I went looking for the source of this noise and found that it was coming from a sheep in a field about two miles away, across the fields towards Wadderson. I thought the town I came from was more peaceful!

Chris Jenkins 353681

OVING, Manor Road c1955 O118008

CHALFONT ST PETER, The Common c1955 C524010

Freewheeling down this hill...

I lived at Chalfont St Peter as a young boy in the 1960s. One day me and my friends found an old bike that had no chain and no brakes. We hid the bike in the gorse on the common, and every day after school we'd get the bike out and take it in turns to freewheel down the slope seen in this photograph. Then we'd push it back up and someone else would have a go. I would have been seven at the time.

Donald Macdonald 23851

Bell ringing at Dorney

The photograph on the right shows the church I was baptised in, the Church of St James the Less at Dorney. As I child in the 1960s I used to go bell ringing here. We had to climb up the very narrow stairwell, being very careful not to slip, and we practiced every week. There were six bells and I rang Number 4. Our teacher would stress to us not to break the stay as it was very expensive to replace so I always felt nervous ringing the bell. Goodness knows what it must have sounded like when we were learning, as all of Dorney Reach and Dorney village would have heard us.

Monica Peck 16161

DORNEY, The Church c1955 D87028

Playing on the machinery and dodging cows in Fenny Stratford (now part of Milton Keynes)

I lived in Fenny Stratford as a child in the 1950s. At the end of Staple Hall Road, just a couple of houses down from where we lived, there was a council yard where some heavy machinery was stored, mainly a very large steam roller, a snow plough and some other wonderful giants. Sometimes after school, when the yard went quiet, me and my friends would climb through the fence and play on these things pretending to drive them, they had loads of wheels and levers to pull and turn. It was great fun.

Over the fence at the end of our back garden were two fields where Farmer Howard used to keep cows. There was an avenue of horse chestnut trees where we could get across the field without the cows chasing us, though Mr Howard did. He had bandy legs and would shout and wave his stick at us, but we always made it to the safety of the gravel pits or back home again. I think he was pretty harmless really, and he never stopped us from picking blackberries in the hedges – that was, if the O'Dells had left any behind.

Roger Clarke 127941

> '*He had bandy legs and would shout and wave his stick at us, but we always made it to the safety of the gravel pits.*'

Our 'beach' at old Bletchley

Back in the 1950s, us locals of 'old' Bletchley (which has now been absorbed into Milton Keynes) had a real 'inland seaside', it was great. We used to swim there or just walk across to a lovely clean 'beach', and wherever you dug there was almost pure white sand. Where was it? Beacon Lake, an old flooded gravel pit. The only thing that wasn't very nice was that we had to get changed in amongst the bushes, but most of them were gorse bushes, and they were very prickly. We couldn't go to the end part (where the Argos store is now, on the Beacon Retail Park in Watling Street) because it was thick clay underfoot, and was overgrown with bulrushes, and it was really cold water. Down the main big part of the lake was also dangerous because it was really deep (some older people used to swim right out, but only if they were strong swimmers, because they used to say it was sometimes a bit scary because of a 'pull' in the currents) and in places the water was very cold, but yes, it was our real piece of inland seaside, and we had many, many happy hours there. We all went there mainly together, in a group, and the older people always looked out for the younger ones. We were mainly from the Western Road and suchlike areas. It was safe then, parents never had any cause to worry about their children, not like today! It must have looked weird for anyone driving down the old A5 to see us all crossing the road with big black blown-up inner tubes over our shoulders – we'd be crossing over to where TK Maxx is now, that site used to be a brush factory called 'Beacon Brushes'. I don't think anyone is allowed to swim in the lake now, it's so very deep. But us 'old locals' used to have lovely times there in those days, although it all seems a long time ago now.

Margaret Hogg (née Margaret McCracken) 95271

'The older people always looked out for the younger ones.'

Ice-skating on the frozen lake

Back in the 1950s my uncle John Cooke owned the gravel pit at Bletchley called Beacon Lake in Margaret Hogg's memory (above), along with the brush factory. We lived in Staple Hall Road in Fenny Stratford and used to go on the very same beach. I remember one winter when my brother Colin took me there, as a five-year-old, to ice-skate on the frozen lake, it was great fun too. In the summer we used to play in the piles of old pipes and the wigwams made of wood from the brush factory, probably put there to dry out. John Cooke was a very kind man and allowed access to the pit for swimming and fishing and some people even sailed their dinghies on the lake.

Roger Clarke 122921

Born in Fenny Stratford

Just after the beginning of the war my mother, sister and grandparents moved to Fenny Stratford to be near my auntie Doris (my mother's sister) and to be away from the dangers of London; they came from Dagenham and Hackney in the East End. My grandfather, Captain Walter Bates, had also just been assigned to the security at Bletchley Park. They all lived with my aunt in Church Street until my mother managed to rent a little cottage in Woodbine Terrace, number 8, where I was born – in attendance were Nurse Brinklow, the local midwife, and Dr Gleeve. My parents were Jim and Vera Cusack, but my father was in Burma in the Far East for much of the war. After the war ended my grandparents returned to London, they were lucky that their substantial house was still intact, however my parents' Dagenham home had been destroyed in the air-raids so they decided to stay in Fenny Stratford. It took my father a lot of getting used to the country way of living as he was a real townie, but he managed in the end and worked until he retired for the GPO (telephones).

I was baptised at the Catholic church in Church Street in Fenny, at only a few weeks old, my mother was a wonderful dressmaker and she made my gown from the parachute silk that she had bought in Cowlishaw's haberdashery shop, in Aylesbury Street. My first vivid memory is of being carried to the corner shop at the top of Church Street, I would have been about eighteen months old. I also remember sitting on a high chair in Oliver Wells' shoe shop to be fitted with new shoes, that was at the bottom of Church Street as you turned right into Aylesbury Street. At that time there were more shops in Fenny than in Bletchley Road and everything that you needed could be bought there, it even had a Dolls' Hospital in Victoria Road, where several of my dolls had to be admitted during my childhood!

Just after Christmas in 1951 we moved house, onto the newly built Manor Farm Estate. I started school in 1952 at the little Bletchley Road school at the end of the drive, overlooking the Leon Recreation Ground, where on a Sunday we might go to listen to the Bletchley Town Band play, my Uncle Percy played the trombone. Sometimes we would go to the Central Gardens, and the Salvation Army Band would play there too. When the Manor Road school was opened in 1954, I moved school as it was so close.

A new Catholic church, St Thomas Aquinas, was built in 1956 on the corner of Sycamore Avenue and Manor Road, and I was one of the first children to make their first Holy Communion there in 1957. I remember how big this new church seemed and how every little sound echoed. It was also very cold in the winter, as there was no central heating then.

Next to the Spurgeon Memorial Baptist Church in Aylesbury Street in those days was Dickie Golding's sweet shop; in the summer months he made award winning ice-cream, and the queue for it on a Sunday after all the services was never ending! Whenever there was a birthday party, we would run to the shop with a large pudding basin for him to fill, but we had to remember to take a tea towel. He would put the basin into the freezer for a few minutes to get it really cold then we'd put the tea towel over the basin to keep the cold in and run back home before the ice-cream melted.

As us children got a little older we would go with our parents to the old flooded gravel pits mentioned in the memories on the previous pages, it was indeed like the seaside there with the big sandy banks and boats, however it was also very dangerous if you strayed too far. Everyone enjoyed themselves there, it was the place to go on a hot summer's day. A child living in Fenny Stratford was a happy child, there were lots of places to go and play, and as far as we were aware in safety. The Manor fields were a favourite haunt, we spent hours there, even in the cold snowy winters when it was covered in ice.

Kathleen Roberts 103401

Memories of Wooburn Green from America

My mother, Vera Brown, was born in Wooburn Green in Buckinghamshire and lived at 135 Boundary Road until she came to America to marry my father after the Second World War. (My father was based in High Wycombe during the war.) As my gran and aunts never left the Wooburn area, my sisters and I spent many wonderful summers there. In 1965 (aged eight) I remember passing every glorious daylight hour on The Golf with the wonderful friends we'd met from the village. We had a clubhouse in the overgrown shrubbery along the railroad line that ended at Loudwater. We would run to the clubhouse when a train was coming so we could feel the power of it as it passed, the rush of air whipping the leaves around us as we watched car after car chase each other down the track. Sometimes, as a deterrent, the conductor of the trains would spray hot water at us as a warning to be careful. I remember, too, while passing time on The Golf, some of the older guys (who were there because of my very pretty sixteen-year old sister) taught my younger sister (aged five) and I how to play a game that I believe was called Splits. The idea of the game was for your opponent to toss a switch-blade into the grass, and if it landed standing you had to put your foot there. The first person to lose his balance lost the game. Thinking about these games now, they seem dangerous – they weren't though, because young as we were, back then we were pretty responsible too. Other than Splits we used to catch butterflies on The Golf, and sometimes look for lost golf balls to sell to golfers for a few pennies. Those pennies were like treasures to us, because as soon as we got them in the palms of our sweaty hands we'd run right over to The Barley Mow. We'd hurry around the side to the back and ring the bell on the door to let the proprietor know that someone wanted to buy candy (sweets). I loved Smarties (I used to lick the red ones and rub them over my lips like they were lipstick), Flakes and the strange potato crisps you actually bought with little bags of salt in them that you had to add to the crisps yourself. These are all wonderful childhood memories that grow more special with age. Lovely as they are though, in 1974, when I was no longer a child, I spent another summer in Wooburn Green and fell in love for the first time – and that, my friends, is a story for another day…

Valerie Killigrew 336191

Childhood memories from Nash

My family lived in a quaint cottage at Nash, a village near Buckingham, from 1946-50, when I was a pre-schooler. My father cycled to Buckingham daily all year round. My first word was spoken in that cottage – it was 'visibility', which I had picked up from listening to the wireless! I have two particular memories from those days. One is when a group of children got stuck in the mud of the village pond and attracted many onlookers. The other is of hearing my mother describing a house being 'upside down' when the owners were moving – I was so disappointed to find that the house wasn't standing on its chimney as I had expected!

Anne Burkinshaw 205142

Picking wild violets

When I was a child in the 1950s my friend Jean and I used to pick wild violets in the wood just along the towpath on the right hand side of this photograph of Dorney, in South Buckinghamshire. The wood was a carpet of yellow celandines in spring and the scent from the wild violets was reward in itself. We lived in Dorney Reach so most of our childhood was spent by the River Thames.

Monica Peck 16161

DORNEY, The Reach 1951 D87007

Rolling Easter eggs down West Wycombe Hill, and more

These are some of my memories from my childhood living at High Wycombe in the 1950s. My family lived on Abercrombie Avenue for a while and I remember playing with spinning tops and a whip in the street with groups of kids. There was a woodyard there, and when it closed we used to climb in and play hide and seek all over the piles of wood. On Saturday mornings we would go to a cartoon matinee at The Grand cinema on Desborough Road. The buses didn't run early on Sundays, so after we moved to Booker from Abercrombie Avenue we would walk all the way into town to church. Sometimes we would walk through woods up to Booker Common where there was a pub that backed up to the woods named 'Live and Let Live', which had a hanging sign of a cat staring at a mouse. That message stayed with me! I also recall playing with 'conkers', and rolling Easter eggs down the hill above West Wycombe, near the church on the hill with the Golden Ball on top of its tower. The Wycombe area was a great place to grow up. I now live in the USA, but have been back many times. It has changed so much, but everything does, however the memories of the good times stay.

Maureen Ingram 59571

WEST WYCOMBE, The Pedestal and West Wycombe Hill 1906 53691

1949 onwards at West Wycombe

I will always consider myself fortunate to have been born in West Wycombe as it presented the ideal place for people growing up in the 1950s and 1960s. The village was a dream location and the school was even better, where I had a super set of friends and teachers well managed by Mr Holdbrook the Head. We enjoyed one of the best playgrounds on The Hill that anyone could have wished for.

The summers seemed long to us children in those days. Our activities included constant games of football and cricket at the Pedestal Stadium as well our main passion of train-spotting. West Wycombe Station was open until 1958 and well managed by Percy the Porter who kept our gang in check whilst we were watching the passing trains. When it closed we built a purpose-made camp at the north end of the down platform and watched the world go by with many friends.

My visits to the village are today infrequent but I am delighted to see how little things have changed there, due to excellent stewardship of the National Trust. Even though the station is long gone and our camp is now hidden by trees and bushes, the memory of those great days remains.

Gerald F Rivett 14641

Childhood memories of the village pond

When we were young in the 1930s my friends and I spent many hours catching sticklebacks in the pond at Chalfont St Giles. A fishing net cost tuppence in those days which was regarded as a lot of money, but it was worth every penny!

William Taylor 86581

CHALFONT ST GILES, The Village and the Pond c1965   C498043t

Snowballs and fire alarms at Medmenham

My dad was a sergeant in the RAF, and along with my mum, Jean, my brother Robert and my sister Carol we lived in married quarters in Medmenham in the late 1950s. I remember my friends Roddy Banks and Chris Waillin and the big snowball fight that took place one winter between the North Close and the South Close – we lost. I recall walking for days in the top woods (Hog Wood) and sledging down a big hill there. I also remember the tunnel beneath the Wittington Estate on our walks down to the River Thames. I seem to remember a steep chalk cliff, but there was a pathway down to the river. Twice I fell in and nearly drowned. I went to Danesfield School and one day Roddy and I smashed the stand-alone fire alarm, bringing fire engines from Marlow and Henley. I had the best childhood in the world in an amazing environment, no wonder I appreciate the natural world.

Chris Carr 364841

Childhood pranks on my grandfather's farm at Singleborough, near Great Horwood

I visited Singleborough recently and my grandfather's farm was exactly as I remember it from nearly 60 years ago – but smaller of course. I stood near the door where my grandfather once showed me some newborn fluffy chicks, and the garden still looked much the same as it did when my mother had her photograph taken mowing the lawn as a young woman. I used to visit the farm when I was about 7 or 8 and got up to no good with the children from across the road, making tunnels in the straw bales in the store, putting rat poison in the calves' food (not knowing what it was, of course) and eating cow cakes until I made myself sick. I fished for sticklebacks and put them in the water butt and found them floating on the top the next morning. I picked cowslips, violets and primroses in the hedgerows. I have so many vivid memories that will never die.

Jenny Kevis 271251

My childhood in Marlow

I grew up in Marlow during the 1960s. I have wonderful memories of a really free childhood of bike rides, exploring the woods, rowing a very old boat on the river, even swimming in the river (which my mum never found out about), and just general messing about! We used to go to Marlow Common and play in the trenches, or trek through the woods to Marlow Bottom to make camps, or go down to the end of St Peter's Street to fish. On weekends and holidays we would be out all day. When I go back for a visit I am amazed at how far and wide we kids used to wander! I went to Oxford Road then to Holy Trinity schools. I remember going to see the Beatles' film 'A Hard Days Night' at the Regal, it was fantastic! On Saturday I used to go to a Miss Hogg for piano lessons, she lived opposite where there was a fire station, I think. If there was cricket on we would go and watch with my dad and have a picnic. Marlow is still a lovely town and I especially love the swans and walking by the river of a summer's evening.

Miss M 72321

> *'A really free childhood of bike rides, exploring the woods, rowing a very old boat, even swimming in the river...'*

MARLOW, The River c1955 M35039

MARLOW, From the Lock 1901 47125t

MARLOW, From Lock Bridge 2003 M35701

Aunty Eliza and her son Alf

My Great Aunty Eliza lived in an area of Buckland (near Aylesbury) called Buckland Wharf, in a long, low, white bungalow where time seemed to stand still except that the grandfather clock ticked in her parlour to tell us otherwise. The room was very dark because the blinds were drawn "to keep out the sun". There was a heavily framed picture of her husband on the wall – a severe looking man with a handlebar moustache, who seemed very much the Victorian gentleman. I cannot remember the furniture in her bungalow but I vividly remember the rag rugs on the floor. In her kitchen she cooked over a range, did her washing in an old butler sink and bathed weekly in an old tin bath. She was quite the handywoman and on her 80th birthday she very proudly showed off her latest creation – a bright emerald green knitted petticoat (my cousin and I were told off for having a fit of the giggles when we saw it).

My mother and her cousin Bill would always holiday with Aunty Eliza when they were little. One memorable day they had dressed her "chuckens" who seriously protested about their treatment and were flying round the parlour in a highly agitated fashion. Poor Eliza hated birds and nearly had the vapours, and cried: "You wretched children, git them chucks out of my best parlour right now!" Mum only had bread and dripping for her supper that night as a punishment. She used to play with Bill out in the paddock, at the end of which was a tree that they loved to climb, but they had to be careful because the trunk was surrounded with stinging nettles. One fateful day Bill pushed my mum into the stinging nettles. She was in agony, with tears streaming down her face, but she cried bravely: "It never hurt, it never hurt!" Mum and Bill used to take their penny and walk three miles to get a stick of liquorice or a lollipop 'from the lady who lived up the hill' and then suck on their treat all the way back.

> 'she cooked over a range, did her washing in an old butler sink and bathed weekly in an old tin bath.'

Aunt Eliza' son Alf lived over the road. He more or less lived in his shed, which was his workroom. On one visit we tried to winkle him out of his shed and noticed the sign on the door: 'The man wot lends his tools is out.' So we never asked him for anything! On another visit we saw this sign: 'Plant for hire – hammer 1p, spade 1p – knock for details.' Family legend had it that Alf never took his cap off and even wore it in bed.

Christine Beddows 39781

Lost in Singleborough

In the early 1950s my paternal grandparents built their retirement home at Singleborough, near Great Horwood. They were true Cockneys and fulfilled a dream to retire to the country. I visited them there twice from New Zealand, once in 1962 and then again in 1966, this time with my new husband. His abiding memory is of the day we explored a public pathway across the farmland around the village. On stopping part way to ask a woman at a house exactly where the path went, she replied that she couldn't help us since she was a stranger in the district and had only lived there for 14 years! My husband has retold that story many times over the years.

Anne Burkinshaw 205143

OAKLEY, The Parish Church 1952   065007

Gran Honour of Oakley

I recall as a boy living in Thame Road at Oakley in the 1950s having to pass the church at dusk, having been in the village playing field until late. We had an old lady who had lived next to us, a Mrs Honour, who we called Gran Honour, who had died and was buried just inside the gate of the churchyard. On passing the graveyard in the dark I would call "Goodnight Gran" and run past as fast as I could for fear she might rise up and chase me.

Eric Brooks 122791

'All Clear' at the Post Office

I was born in a cottage at Maids Morton, opposite the Wheatsheaf pub, when our village was greatly different from what it has now become. It was a very pretty old village in my youth. I grew up in the proverbial English village, and they were happy days. I remember Baroness Kinloss, relative to the Duke of Buckingham, dressed all in black, knocking on our door to wait until there were no customers in Mrs Roberts' Post Office. I would be dispatched to the Post Office and run back to our house with the 'All Clear'. After the Baroness died, her house in the middle of the village was pulled down to make way for the new housing estate that stretched right down the length of the village, taking Culley's farm also.

Carole Orpe (née Smith) 363531

MAIDS MORETON, The Post Office c1955 M264010

DENHAM, The Village c1965 D183019

My favourite bridge

I remember this bridge at Denham from when I was little and living in Higher Denham. We often walked into the village this way, past the lovely brick wall and past the hut where we got free orange juice after the war. My grandmother ran The Plough pub which was up the road straight ahead in the photo. My brother once fell in the river near this bridge. We were in the tiny newsagent's shop in the village, and he went out the back door and fell into the river. It wasn't deep and he was soon fished out, but we still tease him about it! I took my children back to Denham (from Canada) a few years ago, and the same lady was still running that tiny newsagent's shop. She seemed old when I was a child and must have been well into her 80s by the time we went back. I had been telling my children about her before we entered, and how she always told us to "Shut that door behind you" before we had got through it. Imagine my surprise when I opened the door and heard that same voice tell me to "Shut that door behind you!". How we all laughed when we left! Nothing much has changed in the village. Seeing this lovely photo reminds me of the wonderful times we spent in Denham as children. I went to school there, to Brownies with Miss Gilby as my brown-owl, to The Plough for Nanny's chips and lemonade, and to our cousins' houses. I miss those days, but am so grateful Denham has been preserved, and we can always go back in time there. One of these days I will take my grandchildren there too…

Jennifer Schinkel 30281

I was evacuated to Buckinghamshire - twice!

Britain declared war on Germany in September 1939, and this country's involvement in the Second World War began. German air-raids and gas attacks were expected imminently, and many children were evacuated out of the cities to the relative safety of the countryside, including my mother, then known as Billie Gwilliam, who recorded this memory for her family of being a wartime evacuee to Buckinghamshire from her home in north London:

'With hundreds of other children I was taken to the station with my gas mask in a box strung round my neck, and a case. Everyone was crying, and none of us knew when we would be home again.

I was billeted with a poultry farmer in Monks Risborough in Buckinghamshire – they already had a girl staying with them called Jean, aged about seven, who was from the East End of London. We called the farmer and his wife Uncle Joe and Auntie Nellie. It was very primitive there, and the food was awful! We had to go to bed lighting our way with a candle, and if we needed to go to the toilet in the night we had to use a potty under the bed. The outside toilet was a board over a hole, and sheets of old newspapers hung on a nail to be used for toilet paper. There was no electricity, no bath or heating, and we just ran wild.

Chickens roamed everywhere, and my lifelong terror of birds really began there, when a cockerel flew up and landed on my shoulder and pecked my head. The old Granny of the family in her long black skirt would kill a chicken for dinner by putting its head under a broomstick and pulling its feet, which always shocked me terribly. Cats lived under the hen houses, and were never fed – when they had kittens, they ate them.

We were put into the local village school, which was about a mile away, and we had to walk there in all weathers. On my first day at school I was put into the front row, and was so overwhelmed by everything that I wet my knickers. I was put into the corner in disgrace, and made to stand in a tray of sand!

We were mimicked because of the way we spoke, especially Jean, who had a very pronounced Cockney accent, and I lived for letters from my mother. I was only five, and terribly unhappy about being separated from my family. It is a memory that I will always remember as a very dark time in my life.

When the expected attacks in the early phase of the war failed to materialise, many of the evacuated children were sent back to their homes. I was so pleased to get back to my parents, but we lived in London and it wasn't long before the Blitz started. I was evacuated out of the city once more, again to Buckinghamshire and this time to Princes Risborough, but this time my mother, aunt and cousin Roger all came too, to be safely out of London. My father stayed in London throughout the war, where he worked by day as an army vehicle maintenance instructor at a technical college and at night on voluntary fire-watching duties; he had to spend part of the night posted on high buildings, such as the top of church towers, looking out for fires caused by incendiary bombs, which he would fight with a stirrup-pump to prevent them spreading.

This second period of evacuation at Princes Risborough was a much happier experience. Our 'home' was with a lady whose husband was in the army. There were three boys in the family and an only daughter, Janet. It was a nice big house with an orchard and a pretty garden, fairly near a railway line. Again I had an 'Auntie Nellie', but this one was a kind and homely woman, and I came to love her dearly. My mother and aunt got jobs in a local nursing home – Mum was a cook there, and my aunt was a housekeeper. My cousin Roger and I went to school with the other children.

PRINCES RISBOROUGH, High Street c1955 P282010

Every Sunday we had our hair washed and all our clean clothes were laid in piles at the end of our beds. I shared a bed with Janet, and the boys all bunked together. Every so often my father would come and visit us, and we were as contented as it was possible to be. However, I missed my grandparents, who lived in north London and resolutely stayed there throughout the war.

One game that we played was putting pennies on the railway track near our house, hiding, and then when the train passed we picked up the coins which were now twice their original size. This now seems a very silly thing to do, but we had no fear at that age. We also made fires, and twisted dough round twigs to cook over the flames, which tasted really good. We were always hungry during the war, because of the food rationing! Food was scarce, and we all had ration cards. Even clothes were rationed during the war and everyone had to 'make do and mend'. Strangely, elastic was also very scarce! My knickers had either old elastic to hold them up, or buttons. All our sweaters were patterned with either stripes or squares, or sometimes Fair Isle pattern, because they were all what we would now call 'recycled' – made out of unpicked old garments. Shoes were the most difficult things to replace when they were worn out, or when we needed bigger footwear – I usually had them a few sizes too big, and wore them with two pairs of socks to make them last.

One of the highlights of our stay with Auntie Nellie was the weekly dance at the WI Hall. We all went – the children danced as well, and as there were no men around, women partnered women.

I remember hot sunny days, filled with happy times with lovely people, and the war seemed not to touch us.'

Contributed by Julia Skinner, on behalf of her mother Billie Gwilliam (now Billie Willcocks) 364881

One of my boots is in Banks Pond!

In 1944 myself and my two brothers were evacuees in Haddenham, and it was one of the best years of my childhood. We lived with an old couple named Mr and Mrs Saw in a house, I think it was named Dolly Cote House and was next to a farm. This was a long time ago now, but one thing I know is that one of my boots is in Banks Pond in the village, as one of my brothers threw it in there. If Banks Pond has not been drained it has been in there ever since!

Len Friday 213971

'*It was one of the best years of my childhood.*'

HADDENHAM, Church End Green 1951 H375006

HADDENHAM, Banks Pond c1960 H375036

Medmenham during the war

I was born in 1942 and my first memories are of the Dog and Badger pub in Medmenham, near Marlow, where I lived for six years following my birth, with my mother and my grandparents, John and Lillian Nye. The pub was my home, almost, from birth. During the war a couple of bombs fell on the village, one damaged the Post Office, next to the Dog and Badger, and the other ruined Mr Jones's new house which he'd moved to from London to escape the Blitz! I was told that Grandpa had constructed an Anderson Shelter in the garden of the pub, but when the bombers came over we had to shelter in the cellar because the Anderson Shelter housed black market petrol! A bend in the Thames by Medmenham, apparently, was an excellent guide to the German bombers bound for Coventry, particularly by moonlight.

'Poppital' 252971

The Wendover Spitfire

I spent part of the war in Wendover as an evacuee from the bombing of London. I recall a huge 'thermometer' that was erected on the clock tower at Wendover as part of the local fundraising drive to pay for a Spitfire, it was graduated in pounds sterling with a picture of a Spitfire at the top. We children, and of course the rest of the Wendover community, subscribed as much as we could, as often as we could, in order to purchase our very own Spitfire, as Wendover's contribution to the war effort. I also recall seeing an army tank sliding into a sweet shop on the corner opposite the clock tower. I wonder if any of these wonderful people who made my stay in their village so memorable are still with us today: Mr Mathews of Mathews Bakery, Willy Swilly the pig farmer and Humanist, Mrs Goodson and the railway man with whom I was first billeted, Mr and Mrs Wright, Avril Brackly and 'Buck' Alcott who were close friends of mine, Lady Garner and 'Pinky', and Bruce Hamilton, they were all beautiful people. Then there was my teacher Mr Pentelope, and last but not least, Father Masters, sadly killed in action, who led by example. If any of you are still with us may God bless you, and also those who have passed on.

Edward (Ted) Pace 51291

WENDOVER, Aylesbury Road c1965   W51033p

I was a wartime evacuee to Dunsmore

During the war I was evacuated with my family to Dunsmore in Buckinghamshire and we lived in Appletree Cottage, opposite The Fox pub. I attended Wendover School until I returned to London in 1946. There was another Norris family who ran the one shop in the village but we weren't related. I used to ring the church bell every other Sunday when the Reverend White came to conduct the service. For this I received the princely sum of 3d, or was it 6d, I can't remember exactly. Mrs Eileen Morton lived in the house by the village pond and during the war she was known to have phoned the Air Ministry to tell them she was about to serve dinner and her husband wasn't home! I believe he was a test pilot, from memory. I am still unable to understand how the population of the village at that time could have supported two pubs!

Ken Norris 292691

Raiding the orchard at Akeley

In 1942, during the war, I was evacuated (aged 5 years old) with my mother to Akeley, a small village north of Buckingham. We lived at 3 Chapel End with Mrs Crook. I can remember going to the school on the village square and being allowed to play in the field behind when the weather was fine. My friends were two brothers and a sister from the Jones family living next door at number 2. We used to raid the farmer's orchard for apples until he came running out shouting and chasing us, but I can't recall if he ever managed to catch us. Opposite our house was the Chapel where every Sunday we would listen to the singing of the congregation, although it seemed to me that they sang the very same hymns every week. It was a happy place for me to live as a child but not so much for my mother, who often cried – I didn't realise until I was older that this was due to the effects of the war going on. When I returned to London the war was still raging and our house was bombed in 1944, but fortunately we were in the air-raid shelter at the time and we all came out safely. Some memories are so vivid.

Pete Smith 202809

> *'We used to raid the farmer's orchard for apples until he came running out shouting and chasing us.'*

My childhood memories of Marlow during the war

My brother and I were evacuated to Marlow from London in 1942, when I was six years old. We lived with 'Uncle' Len Roblett , his wife 'Aunt' Rosie and their sons Goosey and Dadle, up Munday Dean. A wealth of memories from that time flood back to me. Saturday morning pictures were followed by sausages from Clarkes the Butchers made by Uncle Len. I remember visits to the sweet shop in old Dean Street, and other visits to the little 'shop' up Munday Dean that was operated in a private house by Mr Edey, where sometimes, presumably using our coupons, we could obtain chocolate and Aunt Rosie's Rhodian cigarettes. Then there were visits to the bathing place where we hired inner tubes for 1 penny to use as rubber rings whilst we were swimming, picnics by the river, and getting up to mischief up Munday Dean, led by our old friend Eddie Ellery! I remember learning to bike ride, and then leaving our bikes at 'Uncle' Jimmy and 'Aunt' Nellie Martin's house while we went into town, and watching the star footballers who were serving with the Black Watch and stationed near Marlow.

Less enjoyable memories include visits to the nurse in Spittal Street for treatment of Impetigo, and sheltering from the 'doodlebug' (flying bomb) which landed at Bovingdon Green.

Gordon Neighbour 73231

> *'Leaving our bikes at 'Uncle' Jimmy and 'Aunt' Nellie Martin's house while we went into town, and watching the star footballers who were serving with the Black Watch.'*

Oh, when sweets came off ration at last!

I lived in Fenny Stratford as a child in the 1950s. A particular memory I have of those days is of Leeson's shop opposite the cinema on Watling Street, it was the first shop that I ever bought anything in. It was when sweets had just come off ration (wartime rationing on sugar and sweets did not end until February 1953) and my mother gave both my sister and I two pence and we walked to the shop where Mr Leeson gave us each a bag with a mixture of small goodies in. It was absolute heaven to us, who had never had shop-bought sweets before.

Roger Clarke 127941

RAF 90 Group Medmenham

After joining the RAF as aircrew in 1950 and being re-mustered as a motor mechanic in 1951, I was posted to RAF Medmenham in 1952 where I was attached to the motor pool. It was a wonderful posting. I have fond memories of my time there, including walking along the river banks and drinking at the Dog and Badger pub in Medmenham village – eagerly going down the road from the camp on pay night to the Dog and Badger was easy, but coming back up the hill with a few pints aboard was the hard part! I also remember on one occasion trying to visit every pub in Marlow and drinking half a pint at each one – I failed!

Happy memories!

Bob Neil 47661

National Service at Medmenham in 1956

I know I was doing my bit for my country at the time, but the time I spent in 1956 doing my National Service at Medmenham will always be in my memory because of the great friends I made at the RAF station there. It was also a beautiful part of the country to be doing my service. I got to meet some of the locals who worked on site at the time and found them very friendly towards this Bermondsey lad from London. At weekends when I was off duty some of the lads I was doing service with and myself would go for walks down the country lanes and really enjoy the countryside. We'd also call in at the local pubs and enjoy the local brews. I wonder if you can imagine what that was like for a Londoner. One thing is for sure, this lad at 69 years of age will never forget Medmenham.

Ted Williams 3151

Oh yes, there were happy days at RAF Medmenham

Medmenham was a beautiful posting and a happy place. I worked in the Orderly Room and also played in the Station Band. Whilst I was there I attended the local dance hall, where I was in great demand as a partner having danced to Silver Medal class before joining the RAF! Now I understand the camp is completely gone, except for ONE of the large gate posts which is in the centre of a roundabout where the entrance was.

Paddy Pollock 6801

Happy memories of JSSC at Latimer in Buckinghamshire...

In 1953 I joined the WRAC and was posted to JSSC (Joint Services Staff College) in the beautiful village of Latimer, what a wonderful time that was. There were two of us arriving at JSSC on that April day and the first place we went to was the NAAFI. Up on the stage were two soldiers playing music, and one of them was the man I was to marry. I was accommodated in Latimer House right at the top with other WRAC personnel, and we all got on famously. The only thing I had problems with were the bats that would sometimes fly out, I was terrified of them. I have photos of us girls sitting up on the roof, which was easy to get to. The village of Latimer had everything we needed outside of the camp – a friendly local pub, a fish and chip café, shops, and a cinema, what more could we ask for! Happy, happy days.

Eva Hamilton 252041

...and more fond memories of JSSC at Latimer and old friends

I was posted to JSSC at Latimer in 1954 from Hadrian's Camp, Carlisle, and after walking from Little Chalfont Station with full kit it was great to walk into the guardroom and have someone stick a mug of tea in my hand, Corporal Homer MM. I also remember CSM Wacky Jones, Major 'Debbie' Reynolds and many others from all services, including the WRAC, it was a great posting. I met my wife to be at one of the Officers' Mess balls, I was a wine waiter and she was a ladies' cloakroom attendant. I wonder how many of the old gang are still around and if they ever get together down at the Queen's Arms in Chesham. I particularly remember Chris Kyvernites, Phil Lewis, Paddy Mcaffrey and Charlie Bailey, whose mate carried him back from a Christmas Dance only to drop him down the steps to their barrack block and break his leg. I also remember Jim Barnes crawling all the way down the drive when he thought he had lost his false teeth. He ruined his best uniform, only to find next day that his teeth were in the loo.

Leonard Bainbridge 234351

Happy days in Latimer

It was only two years or so that I lived in Latimer, from 1959-61, when I was aged 6-8, but it still seems as if the happiest period of my childhood was spent there in one long, endless, glorious summer. My dad was in the army, in the King's Own Scottish Borderers, and was attached to the Joint Services Staff College there, which is now Latimer House, the conference centre. I don't know what my dad's job was, but his office (behind the married quarters and since demolished) was later bombed by the IRA – fortunately this was after we'd moved to Scotland, but Dad's former secretary, 'Aunty Edna' as we knew her (the wife of Chick Allen), was injured in the blast. I remember that Edna and Chick had a grey Alsatian dog called Smokey. She seemed gigantic to us kids and would let us ride on her or rest our heads on her flank as she lay in the sun. She followed us when we played and guarded us, nudging us off the road when a rare motor vehicle came along.

We lived up the hill from the village, at 41 ORMQ (Other Ranks' Married Quarters), now re-named The Ridings. The village itself is unchanged after 50 years, although the sweet shop is no longer there, and not too much is really different in the 'army' area either: the motor pool on the Flaunden road is gone, as are the single soldiers' barracks, but the tennis courts are as they always were, as is the raised field next to them, where the Duke of Edinburgh arrived by helicopter to present medals to some of Dad's ex-colleagues a year or so after we'd moved away. (Going back there for this occasion was the only time we returned to Latimer as children.) Bordering this field was Needham's Farm (as we knew it) and the track leading to the farm from ORMQ is still there. We used to walk along it, through the 'bluebell woods' and into the crop fields where we played kiss chase. We played kiss chase a lot, when I think about it! From the field we could cut through to the Flaunden road where we'd pick blackberries and hazelnuts. Also along the road was an area we called the 'Happy Hunting Grounds', one end of which we named 'Yardley Wood End' and the other, 'Silver Birch Point'. We played Cowboys and Indians there. The area of the bridge over the river, by the weir near the junction with the Chesham-Chenies road below Latimer, is absolutely unchanged to this day! Going there is like time-travel. We used to make rafts out of giant watercress-type plants and float downstream.

CHENIES, The Primary School c1965 C609040

My brother Pete and I attended the wonderful Chenies School, the kids travelling to and fro in a Bedford van driven by a little old man a grey moustache who wore horn-rimmed glasses and a chequered cloth cap. We used to queue up in the mornings under a car port at the end of ORMQ which was full of jeeps and 3-ton trucks – replaced now by new housing. (The army barber we used to go to was somewhere there as well.) I've never forgotten Miss Reddit, our headmistress and my first guiding inspiration in life. You can still see my initials scratched in the brickwork on the front of the school. Apart from the permanently installed play apparatus, Chenies School is almost exactly as it was in our time and a sheer delight to visit again.

New houses now stand at the junction of ORMQ and the Officers' Quarters and the woods between ORMQ and the Officers' Quarters have been thinned out recently, but the pine trees we used to climb and make dens under are still there, as are the 'bread trees' as we called them – are they redwoods? They look as huge to me now as they did as a child. I loved Latimer – still do, and always will.

John Sayer 204840

My idyllic time in Buckinghamshire as a child

In 1954 my army father was posted to the staff college (JSSC) at Latimer in Buckinghamshire after his three years in the Korean war. One of the happier parts of my childhood was spent in a lovely little rented cottage adjoining a farm with a big barn where we could play, and there were chickens and horses for us to enjoy. I think it was on the road out of Chesham. The school I went to was called Long Meadow. We often went to Chesham to feed the ducks, and I also remember visiting the model village at Beaconsfield and going shopping in Amersham. It was a safe and stress-free time for my family, especially after my dad's two years spent as a prisoner of war. Sadly, we soon had to move on to the next place…and then the next…as constant upheaval and change was the norm for us army kids. But I always remember the idyllic time we spent in Buckinghamshire. Lovely memories.

Alison Fowles *287541*

BEACONSFIELD, The Model Village c1955 B609066

BEACONSFIELD, Bekonscot Model Village c1960 B609123

> '*It was a safe and stress-free time for my family, especially after my dad's two years spent as a prisoner of war.*'

CHALFONT ST PETER, Gold Hill Common c1960 C524048

The mock battle at Chalfont St Peter

Gold Hill Common at Chalfont St Peter has an upper flat grassy area and then a sloping area leading down into the town which is covered with scrub. This photo is right on the edge of the upper part. In 1963, when I was a boy of eight, the army came to Chalfont St Peter and laid on an exhibition, I guess this was part of a recruitment drive. They carried out a mock battle with half tracks and guns firing blanks and yellow smoke billowing slowly across the common. If you take the main footpath from Layter's Green Lane across the common (the swings and stuff will be off to your left), there was – and may still be – a hawthorn tree to the right of the path. During the mock battle I lay under that tree with a soldier who was firing a Bren gun. I asked him if I could have any of the spent cartridge shells as a souvenir but he told me that they all had to be accounted for. It was an amazing experience.

Donald Macdonald 23841

Aylesbury Carnival

A big memory I have of living in Aylesbury in the 1960s and 70s was the annual Carnival which we would always watch from the top of Buckingham Road. I remember it being quite a big celebration, with marching bands and a procession of large lorries greatly decorated by the individual clubs, and all the people waving and cheering like mad. We would then follow the procession into town, where the streets were crowded with people, ending up at the Market Square. We'd then visit the Fair through the archway, which was held on the field by the Cattle Market, later to be the site for the Civic Centre. I also remember the 'Hobble on the Cobbles', with loud music and dancing in the evening...but I was always too young to attend!

Vicky Williams 228891

AYLESBURY, Market Square c1955 A84050

DENHAM, The Airfield c1965 D183014

Winch gliding with my father

My father, Edward Wyatt, spent every spare moment he could flying his glider at Denham airfield in the 1950s. We lived in Higher Denham, and as young children my brother, sister and I were taken to the airfield on many a Sunday. We were strapped into the back seat of the glider and off we would go. I remember the winch letting go, and then we soared up to what seemed like the heavens. Once we were up, my father often insisted that we take the controls. My dad also had a small plane, and would take us flying to high altitudes to help alleviate whooping cough (I think). We looped the loop, and felt sure we would fall out of the open cockpit...fond memories! We moved to Canada in 1955, but when my dad passed away in 1983 he requested that he be buried in Denham churchyard. This was where his heart was always, particularly the airfield...

Jennifer Schinkel (née Wyatt) 21861

Where are the beaches?

As a little girl, I always remember going here with my mum, aunt and cousin.

Mum would say "We are going to Burnham Beeches today", and when we got there I could never quite understand where the sand and sea was... I realise now that 'Beeches' meant 'trees'... and not seaside 'beaches'!

Lorna Lewis 7461

BURNHAM, The Beeches c1955 B250002

MARLOW, The Embankment c1955 M35024

Visits to Marlow in the 1930s

My parents had two very good friends in Marlow, and as a result we as children (I was the eldest of six) found it a wonderful haven to be welcomed at their home on countless occasions as we were growing up. We lived in London, and each journey to Marlow was an adventure, going to stay in the 'country'. I always looked forward to going there when the Regatta was on, although as this was held in June my hay fever was always at its worst at that time.

My first memory of visits to Marlow is of being met at the station with 'Uncle' and his bicycle and I was carried on the crossbar while he walked with my parents and me to their bungalow at Munday Dean. The first impression that always met me there was the gasworks smell and when finally the gasworks came down I really felt it a huge miss! It was probably not so for the locals though. I have memories of 'Auntie' lighting the oil lamps in their house and I missed that smell too in later years.

We had lovely picnics by the river, and Auntie would bring down a loaf which she would slice for us and spread with Marmite, and it was heaven! We also used to swim in the river, which was quite dangerous on reflection, as the floor of the river was very uneven and it was easy to swim out of your depth. Of course, people don't swim in the river now due to pollution. The bathing place near the weir was a favourite place too, we spent many a happy day there. There was a man called George who was the attendant. The local schoolchildren all tried for their 20-yard certificate there.

It was also lovely going blackberrying in the woods at Woodend, at the end of Munday Dean. I would never have known country life if I had not known Marlow as a child.

Winnie Jeffers (née Neighbour) 69711

AYLESBURY, The Aylesbury Arm, The Grand Union Canal 1921 70564

Smelly days at Our Lady's School at Corby

When I was young in the 1950s the opposite bank of the Grand Union Canal
as seen in the 1897 photograph 39642p (below) was the site of Frith's, the
builders' supply company. My father was a salesman for them for many years.
The location was called Hilda's Wharf, and in the 1940s and early 1950s some
of Frith's supplies such as bathroom tiles were delivered there by narrow
boat – tiles are fragile and the canal was a smooth ride. Of course Frith's is
long gone, and a row of townhouses now stands on its site.

Doug Caton 10451

AYLESBURY, The Canal 1897 39642p

My father was the manager of the Bull's Head Hotel at Aylesbury

My father was the manager of the Bull's Head Hotel at Aylesbury in the 1950s, Mr Ronald F Williams. I remember sitting with my corgi called Kim in that front bay window looking at the people passing by. I also remember a time when the Italian film star Sophia Loren was staying at the hotel and she joined us for tea as my mother is Italian also, they had a good long chat. How lovely to see this fantastic old hotel again and what a shame it's no longer there – demolished in 1969, the hotel's former site is now the entry to the Hale Leys shopping centre.

Shirley Williams 213051

AYLESBURY, The Bull's Head Hotel c1965   A84082

and so was mine...

My father, Bill Thomas, was one of the last managers of the Bull's Head Hotel at Aylesbury. He helped the police when they stayed at the hotel working on the Great Train Robbery of 1963.

Hedley Thomas 203738

I was a pre-student and nurse at this hospital

I worked at the Canadian Red Cross Memorial Hospital at Taplow from 1954 to 1958.

I lived in the old Isolation Hospital at Cippenham that had been converted to a nurses' home, and we travelled by bus from there to The Canadian. The hospital was always very busy, although it had no A & E. We always seemed to be short-staffed and we had to turn our hand to everything. Working hours were 7.00am till 1.00pm or 4.00pm till 10.00pm, nights was from 10.00pm till 7.00am. We nurses wore a very smart uniform, a royal blue dress, a starched white apron, a white hat and brown flat shoes.

My first ward was the Rheumatic Fever Unit for children, where Professor Bywater was Chief Rheumatologist. The only visiting hours were on Sunday, from 2.00pm till 4.00pm, which was so hard for the little ones. I worked on all the Wards 1 to 13. Wards 12 and 13 were for TB patients and 1 and 2 for the Rheumatic Fever. If you were on night duty you were given two Wards to work, and I frequently had this job. It was a long walk from Wards 1, 2, and 3 to 12 and 13 (some people said it was a quarter of a mile from one end to the other) and NO RUNNING was allowed! Miss Morris was the Matron, a very charming lady. I loved all aspects of nursing and enjoyed Theatre work too. The Sister was from Maidenhead and, as I recall, quite feared. I was lucky as she was extremely kind to me. The Theatre Staff Nurse was a super nurse, I used to watch her and think to myself that she could operate herself any time, she was so efficient and a constant help to the young doctors.

When I spent time on the TB unit, Richard Todd, the actor, came to visit and he signed my apron! Sadly I had to send it to the wash, as was expected of us. This was probably akin to washing Brad Pitt's autograph away nowadays! On the male TB unit, young men who had to stay for quite long periods got up to all sorts of tricks, grease on the door handles being a favourite. At one time I was in a fluster because the Night Sister was very strict and I was behind, and the patients knew that. Three of them put me in a linen bag and pushed me outside into the woods that were at the back of the hospital. When I tipped myself out and rushed back they were all sitting up in bed smiling at me, all the wheels on their beds straight (this was a must in those days), and all temperature and pulses recorded! I loved them.

Valerie Kent 72771

> '*Three of them put me in a linen bag and pushed me outside into the woods that were at the back of the hospital.*'

TAPLOW, The Canadian Red Cross Memorial Hospital c1955 T11001

Mushroom stalks on toast and starched aprons and caps
- more memories of nursing at CRCMH at Taplow

What a blast from the past it was to read Valerie Kent's memories of working at the Canadian Red Cross Hospital at Taplow on the Frith website (above). I must have been at the hospital about the same time as Valerie and I relived every moment as everything came vividly to life as I was reading through her account. I remember that our breakfast whilst on night duty was mushroom stalks on toast. We never did find out who had the mushroom heads! Miss O'Connor was the assistant matron and she seemed to know everyone's name. I only went to Matron's office once and that was with a broken thermometer. You can't compare the throw-away mentality now with the strict regime from those days. Needles were taken to be sharpened and things were reused after sterilising. Other names I remember from that period were Joan Key (Kiwi), Corinne Benfield, Brenda Kent, Mary Mercer and Joan Overton. I lived at Hitcham House with Sister Tutor, Miss Postle, always hovering. If you had a boyfriend she always wanted to know about him. Mrs Wright was the housekeeper and Blackie was one of the ladies in the kitchen. She was always ready to help. If you wanted to stay out after 11 o'clock at night you had to ask special permission and were entrusted with a door key. PTS at Wexham Park and my time at CRCMH were some of the happiest days of my life. I know I am an old fuddy duddy but I still prefer the nursing methods of those days, such as wearing starched aprons and caps and being known by my surname.

Ellen Ford 175881

I was a patient at the Recuperative Home at Farnham Royal (between Beaconsfield and Slough)

I was a patient at the Recuperative Home at Farnham Royal for 6 weeks in 1966 or 1967, recovering from a car crash which badly damaged my right arm. I had to have lessons on how to become left-handed! I went home for the weekends and, after a couple of weeks of doing this, one weekend I decided to drive back on the Sunday night in my 1932 MG J2 two-seater sports car. I had to hide it from the staff by pushing it into some bushes in the grounds! I remember getting four of us patients into it to sneak out and go to the pub, we had all plaster and bandages everywhere. My stay at the Recuperative Home did me the world of good, I was only 21 and had a very uncertain future to face. The staff there were brilliant and helped to set me up both mentally and physically, and I never looked back.

Mike Alderson 338861

FARNHAM ROYAL, The Recuperative Home c1955 F195034

FARNHAM ROYAL, The Recuperative Home, Swimming Pool c1955 F195042

FARNHAM ROYAL, The Recuperative Home c1955 F195057

Meeting my dad out of the Wolverton Works

This photograph from around 1910 shows crowds of men leaving the Wolverton railway works. When I was young in the 1950s, I used to cycle to Wolverton every Friday to meet my dad when he came out of the railway carriage works at the end of the day. When the hooter went, about five thousand men came out the gates. Dad used to buy me sweets from Musket's sweet shop and take me to the indoor market, and we'd have a cup of tea at Ethel's, she ran the tea bar. Then we'd cycle back to Loughton.

Jose Mabbutt 211271

> *'When the hooter went, about five thousand men came out the gates.'*

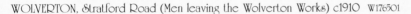

WOLVERTON, Stratford Road (Men leaving the Wolverton Works) c1910   W176501

MAIDS MORETON, The Village c1955   M264006

I did a job here on my first day at work

I can never pass through Maids Moreton without recalling my first
day at work as an apprentice electrician for The East Midlands
Electricity Board, Buckingham. It was April 14th 1958 and I was
assigned to Mr Jack Holland, electrician, and we were sent to
install a lighting point in a rear toilet for 'Mrs Holmes, The Old
Bakehouse, Main Street', and I have never forgotten it. It was the
beginning of a career in the electrical business that lasted until I
retired in 2003, having completed over 45 years in the trade. I can
never forget that address nor the gentleman, now sadly gone, who
gave me my first start on that long 'electrical road'. Thank you, Jack.

Rick Brock 89101

Memories of Aylesbury during the 1960s and 1970s

I have many happy memories of growing up in Aylesbury in the 1960s and 1970s, when it seemed to be a bustling busy town with many little shops. These shops included Weatherhead's book shop in Kingsbury Square (where I loved spending hours looking at the second-hand 10p books in old boxes underneath the tables!) and Baker's toy shop in Buckingham Street, which I would visit with my dad – sometimes he would treat me to some of the little plastic animals that were displayed in a glass case at the far end of the shop, for my farmyard. I also used to visit the 'Pages of Aylesbury' bread shop (also in Buckingham Street) with my mum for our bread and I remember looking longingly at all their cakes displayed in the window. I didn't know then that later in my life I would actually work there as a Saturday girl for three years in the 1970s, until I went to college.

Vicky Williams 228891

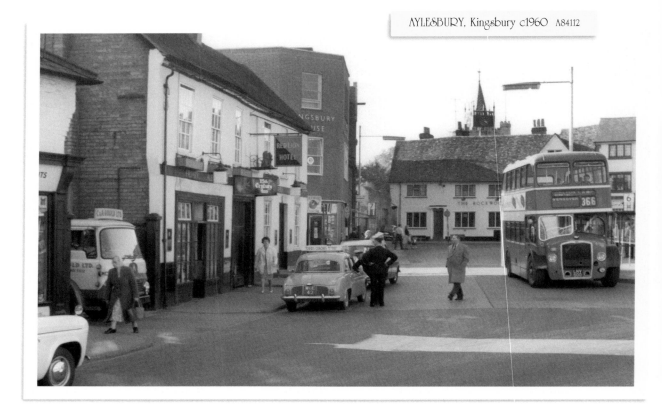

AYLESBURY, Kingsbury c1960 A84112

Bletchley from 1953 onwards

My parents moved to Bletchley from London in early 1953, they first lived in St George's Road before moving to 35 St John's Road when I made my appearance shortly after Christmas. So much has changed since then, but the estate is much like it was in the early years. I have such happy memories of my childhood. I used to love watching the men busy at the brickworks. I think I am the only person that actually liked the smell from the chimneys. What was so good about those days was that everyone was friends with each other and looked out for and cared for each other, nothing was any trouble. I remember going to the local shops in St Mary's, having my hair cut at Vic Shaw's barbers, and getting shopping from David Smith's grocers store – I also remember them getting a BEDFORD CF van for their deliveries, what an advance I thought. I used to save my pocket money to buy Matchbox cars and cardboard roadways for my collection from Bill Price's news shop, where later I got my first paper round.

Behind us at the bottom of the garden was Mr Sidebottom's small farm which had fruit trees and a big chicken run with a shed, the sound of the chickens clucking and the cockerel crowing was childhood magic. The saddest time when his farmland came to be built on was when they felled the 'old man' (a big elm tree), the shape it had grown in looked like a man's head with a beard, and as the tree fell it screamed and cried so realistically. In Buckingham Road we had Elm Farm where we bought fresh milk and produce from Mrs Tomkins, who was always wearing her pinny and wellies, a sight to behold, she was a lovely lady. Across the road was Mr Kemp with his Bengal Farm Dairy, I once got a job with him on a milk round. As you continued down Buckingham Road to the crossroads you had Chandler's Stores, the Co-op in Newton Road, a butcher's, a grocer's shop and an off-licence next to it, then across the road was a haulage yard, I think it was Harris's, and what was Glen Farm, which later became Glen Garage with the farmhouse being the sales offices, part of the old walling is still visible alongside the Tesco store and apartments that now occupy the site. As we continue towards town up Maegors Hill at the top right hand side is now a vet's, this once was the site of a huge banana-ripening warehouse for Fyffes Bananas. Just along from there on the left was another big yard, this was VBA Stevens Fruit and Veg. Moving on a short distance, on the left hand side of the road was Keyes General Stores and the old Bletchley Post Office, and on the right hand side stood a big mansion house at Holne Chase, this was Bletchley Library before it moved to its current site in Westfield Road. As we approached town before the railway was A R & W Cleavers' hardware builders' supplies, then Railway Terrace, both long gone. The former bridge/tunnel from Buckingham Road to Bletchley Road was a low arch two way traffic and footpath connection into town. Once in town besides the shops was once a great market, outdoor and indoor as well as a cattle market and auction rooms. The Co-op Departmental Store was a showpiece and there were many mixes of shops and homes the length of Bletchley Road, I remember the supermarkets at the same time being Fine Fare, Keymarket's, Price Right and Woolworth's. Back then there was a lot for us to do as children and teenagers, we had the Studio Cinema, swimming pool, Central Gardens, cafés, Leon recreational ground, record shops, and we thought nothing of walking to many of the outlaying villages, even walking to Wolverton open-air pool. Great days, great times, so sad they are lost.

Alan Webb 204060

Life at The Stores, Chaloners Hill, Steeple Claydon

I was seven when my family moved to Steeple Claydon from London in 1956. We lived at number 1 Chaloners Hill, otherwise known as The Stores, which my parents ran until the late 1960s. In this photograph the petrol pumps outside The Stores are just visible on the left-hand-side of the road.

Across the road Vic Burrows ran the bakery and we were treated to the smell of freshly baked bread every morning. Mrs Whiting had the newsagent's and Cyril and Ruby Griffin ran the Fountain pub. There were five pubs in Steeple Claydon then, whereas poor old Middle Claydon, East Claydon and Botolph Claydon didn't have one between them. We had nine shops in the village in those days, including a Post Office, and they supplied all our needs. At Austin's you could buy fishing tackle and a penknife and get a haircut if you wanted one. Dennis Robinson, who also ran the Phoenix pub, would mend your bike and he also displayed the latest Raleigh bike in his workshop window. This was torture for us boys - we would gaze at it for hours, making ambitious plans to raise the ten or twelve pounds required to buy it.

STEEPLE CLAYDON c1955   S565008

We vowed to get jobs on the local farms or, when the season came, spend the summer evenings fruit picking at Claydon House. We went fruit picking but five shillings at the end of the week was a long way short of ten pounds and it burnt a hole in our pockets and was soon spent. If anything more exotic than the village could supply was required, the Langston & Tasker bus would take us to Buckingham on Tuesdays and Saturdays.

Steeple Claydon was a proper working village then, self contained, sleepy and slow, it was the tail end of a thousand years of history. It was a wonderful place to grow up. I have happy memories of the village school, the meandering stream that ran just outside the village known as 'the planks', long walks down the Calvert road, and making children's camps that were hidden away in quiet corners. Then there were cricket matches down the recreation ground on summer Sunday afternoons and rowdy football matches on autumn Saturdays, dances at the Library hall (which were always followed by a fight!), church on Sunday for some, chapel for others, and the public bar of the village pubs for the majority.

In 1965 aged sixteen I returned to London, but Steeple Claydon has always remained my home.

Paul Curtis 169861

> 'At Austin's you could buy fishing tackle and a penknife and get a haircut if you wanted one.'

Soggy bread!

Reading the memory of Steeple Claydon by Paul Curtis (above) on the Frith website reminded me of when I was sent on my grandmother's old bicycle from Calvert to the bakery at Steeple Claydon to get a couple of loaves. The bread was placed in one of the old-fashioned paper carrier bags which I hung from the handlebars of the bike to take home. On my way back it rained so hard that the bottom of the bag split, leaving the bread on the road and half a bag dangling from the handlebars!

Patricia Armstrong 285181

The best roast lunches ever, at The Swan in West Wycombe

I worked in High Wycombe in the 1970s as a young man in my twenties and discovered The Swan pub at West Wycombe (you can see its sign on the right-hand side of this pic). Every weekday lunchtime they did a roast dinner and pudding and a coffee for a set price. There was no other menu. I remember the dining room having some big and some small tables. The same people went there for lunch every day, but because I had only been going there two days a week for two years, no-one actually spoke to me yet! The most fantastic roast lunches were served up by two old ladies and a daughter of one of them, I think. I would guess the daughter to be forty and the other ladies to be ancient. It was like school dinners on steroids. Sometimes tourists would call in and you would see them looking for a menu, saying something like "Perhaps a little salad, darling, or some tuna on brown bread?". Suddenly roast lamb and three veg would clatter onto the table in front of them, and they would always be too scared of the old ladies to say anything.

Donald Macdonald 23901

WEST WYCOMBE, High Street 1954   W340016

Shopping in Hazlemere in the 1960s

I was born in Curzon Avenue in Hazlemere (near High Wycombe) in 1953 and moved to Amersham Road in 1958. Hazlemere had a good choice of shops when I was young, including the Post Office and newsagent's, a record shop, a boutique called 'Maggie Mae', a furniture shop, a chemist's, a sweet and toy shop (Duggin's) and a general stores amongst them. There were lots of people about and the shops were always busy. We did all our food shopping in Hazlemere and only went to nearby High Wycombe for other things, where there were bigger stores like Woolworth and Murrays.

From a very early age my mother used to send me to the crossroads to do the shopping for her. Every Friday after school I used to go to Ford's the grocer's with my shopping list for the week, order all the goods, pay for them and then walk back via the sweet shop to spend the 3d (that's about 1p in decimal money) that my mum gave me. Ford's had a grey van which was used to deliver the goods to our house. Often the shopping arrived home before me! Ford's was, in the 1960s, one of the earliest supermarkets and had various offers. My dad won a Mini car in a Heinz soup competition in 1962 and the prize included a case of tins of all 57 Heinz varieties which he gave to Ernie Ford to distribute to his customers. Hazlemere crossroads wasn't that busy with traffic then and sometimes I'd go up there on my scooter or bike with no worries.

Gill Pateman (née Blake) 198511

HAZLEMERE, The Crossroads c1960 H470010

The most interesting barber's shop in the world

Probably just behind the photographer in this view of the crossroads at Hazlemere (H470010) was an old-fashioned men's barber shop. All the old men would go there for a haircut and mums would take their sons too. What the mums never knew is that when you sat in the alcove to have your hair washed, there were numerous naughty pictures that could only be seen from in there. I wonder if any boy ever told his mum what he'd seen?

Donald Macdonald 23891

Memories of High Wycombe 1960-1975

I was born in the Shrubbery Nursing Home at High Wycombe in 1957. We lived in Hazlemere, and I remember going shopping in High Wycombe with my parents on Saturdays in the 1960s. We'd go to Aldridge's for fruit and vegetables and Brazil's (pronounced 'Brazzles') for pork pies and black pudding. Both shops were on the high street opposite one another. I remember eating cockles on a cocktail stick in a little white saucer – and sometimes shrimps – in the Cornmarket. I remember the toy shop – JS Davy's – on the corner of Queen Victoria Road and Easton Street, and also have fond memories of the Murrays department store, I was always fascinated by the wavy canopy that hung above the front entrance. We went to see Father Christmas there several times. Almost opposite Murrays was a narrow street where we used to get kippers and cod's roe, which we ate on Saturday evening whilst watching 'Doctor Who' and the Daleks on television.

As a teenager in the 1970s, I used to buy cheap jewellery from a stall in the Guildhall, records from Percy Prior's (just along from Murrays) and the latest clothes and shoes from a couple of stalls on the Red Lion side of the high street. I remember dark, dingy old Woolworth's too! In those days I had a very dull Saturday job in a bakery in the Octagon – I think it was called Parslow's.

Jayne Smith 204272

WOLVERTON, Church Street c1955 W176022

Picking off the hot crust of bread

I always remember seeing the chimney of King's bakery at Wolverton (in Church Street) smoking away and the lovely smell whilst they were baking the bread. I used to love going into the shop as a child to buy freshly cooked bread and I enjoyed picking the hot crust off on my way home to Mum. Happy memories of my childhood and later years in Wolverton, where I lived for 20 years until 1975.

Susan Travell 206619

Market day in Buckingham

My father was a drover who worked at the cattle market in Buckingham until it closed in the 1950s. His name was Reg Coulton ('Ginger'). I also remember that poultry was sold in a yard further down the street. We kept warm in the winter in the 'Baron's Grill'. Happy days.

Rod Coulton 138531

BUCKINGHAM, Town Hall and Market Place c1950 B280027

BUCKINGHAM, High Street and Cattle Market c1950 B280022

Catching newts at Tylers Green

The building in the background to the right of this photograph with the little spire was my school when I was 11 in 1966. I spent many hours catching newts in that pond in the foreground. It was partly surrounded by a brick and concrete wall and the newts would tuck themselves into little caves.

Donald Macdonald 23991

TYLERS GREEN, The Green c1955 T354005

My school days at Farnham Common

FARNHAM COMMON, The County Primary School c1965 F196013

I remember walking from Hedgerley to the school at Farnham Common in the winter of 1971, only to arrive at the gates and see this view but with the whole car park and playground being flooded. No school today! Sometimes when there was flooding it was a couple of days before the water had drained away. On the left of this photograph is where we used to stand waiting for the door to open for our school disco etc. It was a great school. Teachers I particularly remember were Miss Painter and Mrs Benjamin – she was a great teacher, but unfortunately I never did get the hang of needlework in her lessons!

Pete Cronin 19251

The good old days at Farnham Common school

I started at the primary school at Farnham Common in 1970, I still think it was the best school ever. We had a swimming pool which I thought was so cool, it was never heated though! But I got my width, length and 7 lengths certificates in Assembly. I remember arriving for my first day at the school dressed in a red cardigan and red beret. My, how times have changed. The headmaster at the time was Mr Little, he was a lovely head. I also remember Mrs Benjamin's needlework lessons – yuck! – that Pete Cronin mentioned in his memory of the school on the Frith website (which can be read on the previous page). I remember Mrs Hunter, now she was a cool teacher, and Miss Painter – she taught French and we went to Paris on a school trip with her. We got silver and gold stars for our work if it was good, and if you got three gold stars you went and saw Mr Little and you showed him your work and were praised.

When I was in my first couple of years at the school I recall having a small bottle of milk every morning at break, with a straw in the top. That was fine during the winter but in the summertime the milk was always warm and tasted terrible.

School dinners – OMG! We sat on tables of (I think) 8 and at the end of each table we had servers who went up and got our lunch for us, in those days you were allowed seconds as well! Then every week the seating order changed and everyone moved up a seat to be a server. Things I remember having for school dinners were Spam fritters, chocolate sponge and pink custard, apple and cornflake tart, very green or very white cabbage, and gravy! And there was always fish on Fridays. We always had knives, folks and spoons on the tables and ate off proper plates, not the plastic tray things that children have nowadays. I can also remember being selected to go and do the teachers' washing up after break or lunchtime and eating the biscuits that were left over – no child is allowed anywhere near a staff room these days.

Some of the classrooms had verandahs outside which we were allowed to sit on at break times, we also had a shed on the corner of the field and could get equipment out of it to use at lunchtimes. I also remember the old steel bars we were allowed to climb on, we were all given a week in turn when we could use them. There used to be a cinema in the school hall on a Saturday morning which I remember going to very early on, and then there were the end of term discos, I have happy memories of dancing to that wonderful 1970s' music.

The school itself over the years I was there always felt safe, and moving on to another school at 11 years of age was very scary. I look back over my time there now that my children have grown and gone through school and myself and my husband also work in schools and feel that I was very lucky to have been part of Farnham Common County Primary School. I feel it gave me a good start through my life and taught me a lot about respect, understanding and occasionally I learnt something in the lessons that I had! I have never been back but hope the school continues to thrive through the years.

Sue Bojczuk (née Hailes) 255991

My first day at school

I lived at Oakley (west of Aylesbury) from 1950-58 with my parents, brother and sister and went to the local infants' school, where Miss Kirby was our teacher. In the winter she used to put our morning bottles of milk around the inside of the fireguard in the classroom to thaw, as they would often be frozen after being left outside in the crate by the milkman. We would then have warm milk to see us through until lunch when we'd eat gorgeous meals cooked by Miss Brooks. On my first day at that school I was handed a pair of knitting needles and a ball of orange wool to make a scarf for my teddy. Those five stitches took forever to grow, as I constantly tangled and dropped them but I did achieve the ability to knit eventually and think of that scarf every time I begin a new garment.

Pauline Heywood (née Page) 230991

> '*I was handed a pair of knitting needles and a ball of orange wool to make a scarf for my teddy.*

Watching the building of the M1 Motorway on the way to school

I now live in Australia but as a youngster in the 1950s and 1960s I grew up just outside Newport Pagnell at Tongwell Farm. I well remember the announcement in 1967 that they were going to build a new city called Milton Keynes and the farm would be part of that new city, but before that happened living on Tongwell Farm was a great deal of fun for me and I always had plenty of things to occupy my time. I attended school in Newport Pagnell and usually got there on my bike and went to my grandmother's house (Kate Daniells) in number 34 Spring Gardens. I then left the bike at her house and walked the two hundred yards to the school. With the building of the M1 Motorway (the first section opened in 1959) the access to the road into town was cut off and the main contractors, Laing's, used to ferry us pupils in a minibus both to school and back again in the evening. As a youngster, seeing the road project grow was most exciting, as were the huge Euclids which were the primary machines used for scraping away and levelling the ground.

Bob Anderson 348081

Fun at Oving School

My family lived in Manor Cottage in Manor Road, Oving, when I was born in 1959 (the house seen on the left of photograph O118008 on page 18). I remember Oving being such a friendly village, I knew everyone who lived in the lower half of the village and I was able to walk safely down the road to the village school until it closed in 1968. We pupils then had to travel by bus to the school in North Marston.

There were less than 20 children in Oving's school when it closed. We all played together in the small playground, made camps in the long grass and had little gardens to grow things up above the wall. We played cricket and rounders in the playground and all had to search in the nettles when a ball went over the fence.

Christine Diamond 227971

Memories of Wendover C of E school in the 1950s

I went to Wendover Primary School in the 1950s, when it was situated beside the clock tower seen in the distance of photograph W51033p on page 38. The headmaster was then Mr H J Figg Edgington, who wore his cap and gown always. I had the best time there. We would walk the Heron Path on nature walks, going down through the recreation ground towards the church and pond, and then back past the stream which had sticklebacks and red throats in it. We used to believe that a grey lady haunted the church tower and would pretend that we had seen her and run for our lives. I was in the school netball team and was the shooter. I still have a photo of us all lined up in our black taffeta skirts and yellow tops. We did country dancing in the school hall, '123 Hop to the Polka' and so on. We also used to sit cross-legged on the floor there and listen to records and stories played on a wooden record player. I first read 'Alice in Wonderland' there and Mr Edginton made us promise to read the book again when we grew up – I remembered that much later in my life and purchased two beautifully illustrated copies to share with my grandchildren. The boys would play football at break time and the girls would swing on the climbing frame. There was a big hand bell which had to be rung at break times and we took turns to be bell monitor. We had to go out a few minutes before time and watch the big hands of the clock on the clock tower clunk into place before running around the playgrounds ringing the bell with all our might. It was a very special place.

Glenys Houghton 147641

Starstruck at Bletchley!

In 1963 when I was 15 I left Bletchley Road Secondary Modern School, and went to work at Moss's, in Fenny Stratford. I thought it was great to earn £3 a week, I did a lot with that. I used to go to lots of dances each week, there were loads to go to at various venues – there was the Palace (or Palais de Dance) at Wolverton, with dances twice a week, Murlsey village on a Friday, and the Wilton Hall in Bletchley on both Wednesday and Saturday. We had a job deciding where to go, it was mainly the Wilton Hall that won, because it was in walking distance from home and so there were no fares to pay out for. We used to regularly see the Hollies, the Searchers, Gerry and the Pacemakers, Brian Poole and the Tremeloes, the Animals, even Lulu, she did her debut gig there. They were great days. Yes, there was a bit of trouble some weeks, but nothing major like today's youths get up to. Loads of 'big-ish' name groups played in Bletchley, people came from miles away to see these bands. It was chaos when the Rolling Stones came there. I used to have to work till nearly 6 o'clock on a Saturday evening so I couldn't have got anywhere near the Wilton Hall to queue up to see them, BUT I did get a quick glance at the Stones on my way home from work, they were sitting in the Mokaris café eating beans on toast – well, they were no different from most people, were they! For about 2-3 years I always left my autograph book in the ticket office of the Wilton Hall where we paid to go in, it was signed by all the stars that played there, but after the Stones played there, everyone's books just went missing, we all had same suspect in mind about who had taken them, but never mind, it was many years ago now.

It brought back many happy memories writing about all that on the Frith website.

Margaret Hogg (née McCracken) 95081

The Wolverton Palais

I remember the 'Palais de Dance' in Wolverton in the 1960s, they put on some great bands there. We used to come up from Fulham in London seven or eight times a year to go there. The people of Wolverton were some of the friendliest people we ever met. There were always seven of us on scooters or in cars and the people always welcomed us, which was a lot different from some of the other towns and villages we visited! One Saturday night we didn't have anywhere to stay so we went into the police station in Wolverton to see if they knew of anywhere. The desk sergeant sent us across the road to a garage that had four coaches parked up there. He said we could sleep in the coaches as long as we didn't make any mess or noise and were out of the coaches by 9.00am. Can you imagine that happening today! Thank you, the people of Wolverton of the 1960s, you were wonderful to us.

Paul Overton 247721

Work and play for a teenager at High Wycombe in the 1950s

I arrived at High Wycombe in 1946, as a young girl from Scotland. I attended St Bernard's Convent school, which was situated in a very large old house on the London Road, across from The Rye. We wore school uniforms, originally in a green colour but they changed to maroon later. The nuns were very strict, but we got a good education. After I left school I worked on Frogmoor. My first job was at The Repertory Theatre, I was a secretary for the director, a Mr Gibson. Then I changed jobs and worked for an accountant, Mr Rowland, on Frogmoor. He was a great man to work for. We had no adding machines in those days, we totalled all the books with a pencil and our brains. I moonlighted at The Palace Theatre, also on Frogmoor, as a waitress and an usher. I was saving money to go to the USA where my brother and sister were. I liked Frogmoor! The buses all circled around it, it was full of activity. There was a newsagent's there where I used to buy cheese rolls on my lunch hours, and Aero bars for my boss (his favourite). There was a shoe shop on the corner where as kids we bought our Clarks sandals. I wandered around town on my lunch hour, often cutting through a lane by Frogmoor to get to the Murrays store, or I went through the parish church path to High Street. I liked to go into Lyons for tomato soup and a crusty roll, and a dish of ice-cream on my way. Also the bookstore on High Street was a favourite stop. I had a friend who worked at The Bucks Free Press office and might stop in there too. I went to the Town Hall dances on weekends, and also the dances held at the Liberal Hall, down from the Town Hall, which were on Tuesdays, I believe. We had fun in those days (the mid 1950s). I remember hearing Bill Haley's 'Rock around the Clock' in a film I saw in a cinema (The Rex?) right by Frogmoor, some people got up in the aisles and danced to it. I also heard Elvis Presley for the first time in a cafeteria across from the train station, but I can't remember its name. It was a white 2-storey building and they played music through loudspeakers. When his record 'You Ain't Nothing but a Hound Dog' came on it was so unusual that everyone paid attention and listened to it, and of course we know what a legend Elvis became. I have so many memories of Wycombe...a particularly vivid one is of coming home from work in a double-decker bus with the fog so bad that the conductor got out and walked in front of the bus with a flashlight, and led the driver slow like a snail.

Maureen Ingram 59571

> '*When his record 'You Ain't Nothing but a Hound Dog' came on it was so unusual that everyone paid attention and listened to it.*'

The Mod wall at High Wycombe

In the early to mid 1960s High Wycombe Town Hall was a wonderland for the emerging music scene. On Tuesday nights for 7 shillings and 6 pence you could see improbable acts like the Rolling Stones, the Who, the Animals, the Yardbirds, the Spencer Davis Group and so on, even on one momentous occasion the Ike and Tina Turner Soul Review. I wonder how many local people from that time remember how we young oiks would gather beforehand at 'the Mod wall' surrounding the library, on the corner of the High Street and (I think) Amersham Hill Road.

Steve Shearsby 224811

'For 7 shillings and 6 pence you could see improbable acts like the Rolling Stones, the Who, the Animals, the Yardbirds, the Spencer Davis Group and so on.'

PRESTWOOD, The Chequers c1965 P281007

Picking cherries at Prestwood

In 1956, at the age of 16, I remember picking cherries on the trees shown just to the left of this photograph of Prestwood while being too shy and embarrassed to acknowledge the presence of my first 'girlfriend', Valery, on her bike below. The Chequers pub at Prestwood was my father's local from the mid 1920s until the mid 1980s. He hardly missed an evening's visit there during the whole of that time, so the Chequers became a rather 'looming' object throughout my childhood, rather like a third (naughty) parent. But it did provide the odd bottle of Vimto and packet of Smiths crisps to me throughout that time!

Roy Taylor 9001

Haircuts at Sherington (between Olney and Newport Pagnell)

Just before the 1960s transformed our innocent lives, us village boys at Sherington had a limited choice of tonsorial art; indeed you could count the number of available haircuts (styles wasn't a word used for men or boys) on the fingers of one hand: Short Back & Sides, Square Neck, Feather Neck and Crew Cut.

Short Back & Sides was the standard cut for 90% of the male population and had been forever as far as I could tell. It left only the crown hair, the length of which to be individually determined, either long, medium or short, and a finishing touch of Brylcream for the men was a must to spruce them up. Square Neck and Feather Neck were pretty much the same thing, with the finish at the nape of the neck being either squared across with the clippers or feathered. The Square Neck was a Teddy Boy cut – Elvis was the role model, so the top was usually long and quiffed. With both these styles the biggest difference from the Short Back & Sides was the tight hairline around your ears. Crew Cuts were about, but were really a 'Yankee' thing and were few and far between in Sherington. The only bloke I knew in the village with one was Slick Slater.

For me, both as a boy and a young teenager, hair cutting had two crucial matters associated with it and in truth both were out of my control: who was going to do it and what was it going to look like. My father was the village expert in trimming dogs (although his normal occupation was a butcher). He had a set of clippers and on Sundays various mutts would arrive for a trim, some being brought to him from as far afield as North Crawley and Newport Pagnell. The dogs and Dad would disappear into the tin shed in our garden. (As an aside, it was on these occasions during my childhood that I learnt that the expression 'y'bu**er' should be used after such doggie commands as 'sit still' and 'get up'… and that they had to be growled deeply and slowly rather than said, otherwise the dog would obviously not understand.) Dogs? Boys? What's the difference? None at all, according to my father. Clippers cut hair on whatever creature they were applied to. All I will say is that you do not need to experience the feel of hand clippers on your hair to empathise with the sitter; just compare the difference between cutting paper with sharp scissors and tearing it.

Dad knew all about what shape a dog's coat should be. Boys were different, so he adapted and adopted the pudding basin technique, which involved putting an upturned ceramic bowl on my head as a guideline. All the hair showing below it was clipped off as close as possible and the bowl was removed, and then all the hair above the basin line was shortened with various utensils, including scissors, razor combs and the clippers. All this was undertaken using the same 'sit still' command he gave to his canine clients… I really felt like a dog. What did it look like? Well, Dad admitted I never turned out as good as a dog. So whilst I already felt like a dog, I probably looked worse than one. Blood, sweat and tears finally persuaded Mum to relieve Dad of this duty. The blood and tears were mine; the sweat was Dad's.

I think that having Dad to introduce me to the pleasures of the barber's art was just a cunning ruse to make me go to Uncle Ben, who cut hair on a regular basis as well as doing his main job as the village carpenter and handyman. In normal circumstances the thought of Uncle Ben cutting my hair would have been bad enough, but given a choice of Dad or an alternative… the alternative had to be better, and Uncle Ben did have electric clippers. I didn't quibble about moving my custom to him.

Uncle Ben was a bachelor and I guess his haircutting business was his opportunity to chat whilst making a few bob on the side. He held court in the kitchen of his cottage and you needed an appointment. That is to say, Mum would have made the arrangements, then at the last minute, to avoid excuses, she gave me a shilling and sent me off with instructions to go straight to Uncle Ben's. Uncle Ben had all the gear… a big chair with a boy box to raise you up to men's height, mirrors to look at yourself whilst he cut away, waiting chairs, magazines or comics, Brylcream and 'Tonic', which smelled of ladies' perfume and which was only applied to men upon request.

Uncle Ben would say "Up y'get air'Alan, 'ow d'ya want it?". I would pause and perform some badly acted thought, then reply "A Square Neck please, Uncle Ben". Uncle Ben now avoided eye contact and his response would be "Are y'a sure y'ur Mum ses that's all right air'Alan?". "Yep", I'd reply, with fingers crossed. And so the cutting and shaping and questioning about what I was up too would commence… No basin and no razor comb, just the

> 'Crew Cuts were about, but were really a 'Yankee' thing and were few and far between in Sherington. The only bloke I knew in the village with one was Slick Slater.'

buzz of the electric clippers and the snipping of sharp scissors. I swear to this day you could feel the cold scissors cutting the square across the nape of your neck. Without any blood, sweat or tears the job was done. I would walk home with the wind whistling around my newly exposed ears, feeling like a rock star. What did it look like when I put a mirror behind my head? Uncle Ben had not been that silly – I looked like a boy with a Short Back & Sides; in fact, exactly what Mum had arranged with him, and I fell for it every time. I was just like all the other boys in the village, we knew Uncle Ben was better than our dads and each time we went to Uncle Ben's he convinced us we would get the cut we wanted.

Eventually we grew up enough to get our hair styled in Newport Pagnell, just in time for the Beatles to hit the scene – and then we all wanted mop-top haircuts, just like the Fab Four.

Alan Garratt 165791

The people in this photo...

This photograph of the Cornmarket in High Wycombe pictures my father-in-law, Guilford Emery (now deceased), his daughter Jen (now deceased), and one of his sons, my brother-in-law David Emery. We first discovered the photograph in what used to be the Safeways supermarket (now Morrisons) in High Wycombe, where a framed copy of it hangs on their wall by the checkouts. I had shopped there but never noticed it until another local spotted the family. We have had lots of discussions about the picture and where the remaining members of the family were when it was taken. I purchased a printed copy of it from The Francis Frith Collection and it hangs on our wall, where it always sets up a talking point.

Mrs Maureen Emery 193471

HIGH WYCOMBE, Cornmarket 1951 H84064

NEWPORT PAGNELL, North Bridge from the Play Pen 1956 N62050

This is me when I was a lad!

The lad leaning on the wall in this photograph was John Cook, whose father was a policeman in Newport Pagnell, the guy to the left in the dark suit is me, and the lad sitting on the pillar (to the right) was David Ashworth, son of Major Ashworth, who lived in Silver Street.

Anthony Burt 53331

I lived here!

These were Elmwood Cottages in the Worminghall Road at Oakley. I was born in the far end house, and lived my first 25 years in the 8th semi along. My mum and dad would have had our house since new. It seems odd to think that we were probably at home when this photograph was taken in the mid 1950s. These cottages were demolished in 1984 to make way for brand new houses. The lovely Elm trees that used to stand in front of the houses sadly got Dutch Elm Disease in the 1970s and had to be felled. Just in the foreground on the left of this view is the village garage that was owned and run by Aubrey Bristow, and to the right, just out of picture is the Royal Oak pub, I remember the landlord as being Fred Welford for many years whilst I was growing up.

Andrew Kinch 36201

OAKLEY, The Village c1955 065003

I lived here for the first 25 years of my life

I lived at the house just at the top of this photograph from my birth in 1944 until I was 25 years old. The outbuildings can clearly be seen in the adjoining field to the family home. I spent all my childhood years playing with my brother and friends here. . I used to love watching the working barges going through the locks. My grandfather kept The Three Locks (known then as The New Inn) as its publican for 16 years, in the days when the barges were horse-drawn.

Stephanie Mcpherson 43251

STOKE HAMMOND, The Three Locks c1965 S566012b

The sound of the siren

I can remember walking along Sycamore Road at Amersham on the Hill with my mother in the 1960s. It seemed to me that the siren on the corner always sounded when we walked past the Regent Cinema. It was the old air-raid siren, but, by this time, it was used to call out the fire brigade. I can recall walking underneath the two trees in this picture. When they were finally felled, they were found to be rotten to the core. The church and the small tin hall on the left of this view were demolished, I believe. There is a modern church on this same site today, and the Regent is a supermarket.

Susan Benwell 278981

> *'It was the old air-raid siren, but, by this time, it was used to call out the fire brigade.'*

Where the name Heelands originated

Heelands is an area within the parish of Bradwell, an old village that is now part of Milton Keynes. I was told a tale by Mrs Lester of Bradwell about where the name of Heelands originated. The story goes that one day the lord of Bradwell Manor had visitors from Scotland staying, and early one morning as they looked out of their bedroom window and looked across the fields towards Heelands they remarked how much the scenery reminded them of home and the 'Higlands' of Scotland, and this is how the name became.

Linda Sholl 106341

AMERSHAM ON THE HILL, Sycamore Road c1955 A373036

Francis Frith
Pioneer Victorian Photographer

Francis Frith, founder of the world-famous photographic archive, was a multi-talented man. A devout Quaker and a highly successful Victorian businessman, he was philosophical by nature and pioneering in outlook. By 1855 he had already established a wholesale grocery business in Liverpool, and sold it for the astonishing sum of £200,000, which is the equivalent today of over £15,000,000. Now in his thirties, and captivated by the new science of photography, Frith set out on a series of pioneering journeys up the Nile and to the Near East.

He was the first photographer to venture beyond the sixth cataract of the Nile. Africa was still the mysterious 'Dark Continent', and Stanley and Livingstone's historic meeting was a decade into the future. The conditions for picture taking confound belief. He laboured for hours in his wicker dark-room in the sweltering heat of the desert, while the volatile chemicals fizzed dangerously in their trays. Back in London he exhibited his photographs and was 'rapturously cheered' by members of the Royal Society. His reputation as a photographer was made overnight.

By the 1870s the railways had threaded their way across the country, and Bank Holidays and half-day Saturdays had been made obligatory by Act of Parliament. All of a sudden the working man and his family were able to enjoy days out, take holidays, and see a little more of the world.

With typical business acumen, Francis Frith foresaw that these new tourists would enjoy having souvenirs to commemorate their days out. For the next thirty years he travelled the country by train and by pony and trap, producing fine photographs of seaside resorts and beauty spots that were keenly bought by millions of Victorians. These prints were painstakingly pasted into family albums and pored over during the dark nights of winter, rekindling precious memories of summer excursions. Frith's studio was soon supplying retail shops all over the country, and by 1890 F Frith & Co had become the greatest specialist photographic publishing company in the world, with over 2,000 sales outlets, and pioneered the picture postcard.

Francis Frith had died in 1898 at his villa in Cannes, his great project still growing. By 1970 the archive he created contained over a third of a million pictures showing 7,000 British towns and villages.

Frith's legacy to us today is of immense significance and value, for the magnificent archive of evocative photographs he created provides a unique record of change in the cities, towns and villages throughout Britain over a century and more. Frith and his fellow studio photographers revisited locations many times down the years to update their views, compiling for us an enthralling and colourful pageant of British life and character.

We are fortunate that Frith was dedicated to recording the minutiae of everyday life. For it is this sheer wealth of visual data, the painstaking chronicle of changes in dress, transport, street layouts, buildings, housing and landscape that captivates us so much today, offering us a powerful link with the past and with the lives of our ancestors.

Computers have now made it possible for Frith's many thousands of images to be accessed almost instantly. The archive offers every one of us an opportunity to examine the places where we and our families have lived and worked down the years. Its images, depicting our shared past, are now bringing pleasure and enlightenment to millions around the world a century and more after his death. For further information visit: www.francisfrith.com

Index of Photographs

FRITH PRODUCTS & SERVICES

Francis Frith would doubtless be pleased to know that the pioneering publishing venture he started in 1860 still continues today. Over a hundred and forty years later, The Francis Frith Collection continues in the same innovative tradition and is now one of the foremost publishers of vintage photographs in the world. Some of the current activities include:

INTERIOR DECORATION

Today Frith's photographs can be seen framed and as giant wall murals in thousands of pubs, restaurants, hotels, banks, retail stores and other public buildings throughout the country. In every case they enhance the unique local atmosphere of the places they depict and provide reminders of gentler days in an increasingly busy and frenetic world.

PRODUCT PROMOTIONS

Frith products are used by many major companies to promote the sales of their own products or to reinforce their own history and heritage. Frith promotions have been used by Hovis bread, Courage beers, Scots Porage Oats, Colman's mustard, Cadbury's foods, Mellow Birds coffee, Dunhill pipe tobacco, Guinness, and Bulmer's Cider.

GENEALOGY AND FAMILY HISTORY

As the interest in family history and roots grows world-wide, more and more people are turning to Frith's photographs of Great Britain for images of the towns, villages and streets where their ancestors lived; and, of course, photographs of the churches and chapels where their ancestors were christened, married and buried are an essential part of every genealogy tree and family album.

FRITH PRODUCTS

All Frith photographs are available Framed or just as Mounted Prints and Posters (size 23 x 16 inches). These may be ordered from the address below. Other products available are - Address Books, Calendars, Jigsaws, Canvas Prints, Postcards and local and prestige books.

THE INTERNET

Already ninety thousand Frith photographs can be viewed and purchased on the internet through the Frith websites and a myriad of partner sites.

For more detailed information on Frith products, look at this site:
www.francisfrith.com

See the complete list of Frith Books at: www.francisfrith.com
This web site is regularly updated with the latest list of publications from The Francis Frith Collection. If you wish to buy books relating to another part of the country that your local bookshop does not stock, you may purchase on-line.

For further information, trade, or author enquiries please contact us at the address below:
The Francis Frith Collection, 6 Oakley Business Park, Wylye Road, Dinton, Wiltshire SP3 5EU.
Tel: +44 (0)1722 716 376 Fax: +44 (0)1722 716 881   Email: sales@francisfrith.co.uk

See Frith products on the internet at www.francisfrith.com

FREE PRINT OF YOUR CHOICE
CHOOSE A PHOTOGRAPH FROM THIS BOOK
+ £3.80 POSTAGE

Mounted Print
Overall size 14 x 11 inches (355 x 280mm)

TO RECEIVE YOUR FREE PRINT

Choose any Frith photograph in this book
Simply complete the Voucher opposite and return it with your remittance for £3.80 (to cover postage and handling) and we will print the photograph of your choice in SEPIA (size 11 x 8 inches) and supply it in a cream mount ready to frame (overall size 14 x 11 inches).

Order additional Mounted Prints
at HALF PRICE - £12.00 each (normally £24.00)
If you would like to order more Frith prints from this book, possibly as gifts for friends and family, you can buy them at half price (with no additional postage costs).

Have your Mounted Prints framed
For an extra £20.00 per print you can have your mounted print(s) framed in an elegant polished wood and gilt moulding, overall size 16 x 13 inches (no additional postage required).

IMPORTANT!

❶ Please note: aerial photographs and photographs with a reference number starting with a "Z" are not Frith photographs and cannot be supplied under this offer.

❷ Offer valid for delivery to one UK address only.

❸ These special prices are only available if you use this form to order. You must use the ORIGINAL VOUCHER on this page (no copies permitted). We can only despatch to one UK address.

❹ This offer cannot be combined with any other offer.

As a customer your name & address will be stored by Frith but not sold or rented to third parties. Your data will be used for the purpose of this promotion only.

Send completed Voucher form to:
The Francis Frith Collection,
19 Kingsmead Business Park, Gillingham,
Dorset SP8 5FB

Voucher for **FREE** *and Reduced Price Frith Prints*

Please do not photocopy this voucher. Only the original is valid, so please fill it in, cut it out and return it to us with your order.

Picture ref no	Page no	Qty	Mounted @ £12.00	Framed + £20.00	Total Cost £
		1	Free of charge*	£	£
			£12.00	£	£
			£12.00	£	£
			£12.00	£	£
			£12.00	£	£
			£12.00	£	£

Please allow 28 days for delivery. Offer available to one UK address only

* Post & handling		£3.80
Total Order Cost		**£**

Title of this book . . . .

I enclose a cheque/postal order for £ . . . .
made payable to 'The Francis Frith Collection'

OR please debit my Mastercard / Visa / Maestro card, details below

Card Number:

Issue No (Maestro only):   Valid from (Maestro):

Card Security Number: Expires:

Signature:

Name Mr/Mrs/Ms . . . .

Address . . . .

. . . .

. . . .

. . . . Postcode . . . .

Daytime Tel No . . . .

Email . . . .

Valid to 31/12/16

Can you help us with information about any of the Frith photographs in this book?

We are gradually compiling an historical record for each of the photographs in the Frith archive. It is always fascinating to find out the names of the people shown in the pictures, as well as insights into the shops, buildings and other features depicted.

If you recognize anyone in the photographs in this book, or if you have information not already included in the author's caption, do let us know. We would love to hear from you, and will try to publish it in future books or articles.

An Invitation from The Francis Frith Collection to Share Your Memories

The 'Share Your Memories' feature of our website allows members of the public to add personal memories relating to the places featured in our photographs, or comment on others already added. Seeing a place from your past can rekindle forgotten or long held memories. Why not visit the website, find photographs of places you know well and add YOUR story for others to read and enjoy? We would love to hear from you!

www.francisfrith.com/memories

Our production team

Frith books are produced by a small dedicated team at offices near Salisbury. Most have worked with the Frith Collection for many years. All have in common one quality: they have a passion for the Frith Collection.

Frith Books and Gifts

We have a wide range of books and gifts available on our website utilising our photographic archive, many of which can be individually personalised.

www.francisfrith.com